Also available from Westcountry History:

Dorset by Peta Whaley

WESTCOUNTRY HISTORY

SOMERSET

Muriel Searle

venton

New paperback edition ©2002 by **venton**, an imprint of:
intellect Books, PO Box 862, Bristol BS99 1DE

A previous edition of this book was published as
Somerset Green and Pleasant Land by Colin Venton ©1975 Muriel Searle.

All rights reserved. No part of this publication may be reproduced, stored
in a retrieval system, or transmitted, in any form or by any means,
electronic, mechanical, photocopying, recording, or otherwise, without
prior permission.

ISBN 1-84150-802-0

Designed, edited and typeset by May Yao and Daniel Carpenter

Cover photograph ©2002 May Yao and Daniel Carpenter

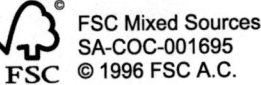
FSC Mixed Sources
SA-COC-001695
© 1996 FSC A.C.

Printed and bound by 4edge Ltd, Hockley. www.4edge.co.uk

Contents

	Introduction: County of Contrast	7
1	Saints and Sheepskin Boots	13
2	Philanthropists and Factories	31
3	Battlefields and Burnt Cakes	39
4	Red Apples and Rough Justice	49
5	Marsh-Men and Milk Churns	61
6	Danes and Dairymaids	71
7	Four B's and the Severn Sea	79
8	Cinderella and Sandcastles	89
9	Benedictines and Babycham	97
10	Singing Boys and Ringing Swans	103
11	H. G. and the Hag	115
12	Alfred and the Archangel	121
13	Saxon Kings and Strawberries	133
14	Slaves and Sunday Schools	141
15	The Curate and the Cavemen	149
16	Fairy Toot and Fat Trout	153
	Conclusion	161
	Acknowledgements	164

Introduction
County of Contrast

CONTRAST is the keynote of Somerset, and nowhere is it more marked than in the central part of the county: high hills split by spectacular natural ravines, and flat peaceful moorlands whose heart is still remote; lush dairying pastures, and important yet unobtrusive industries whose names are household words: the cradle of English Christianity, and scenes of bloodshed and legalised murder; modern man in his cars and touring coaches and ancient man existing in dark hyena-haunted caves or in primitive huts poised on wooden platforms above swamps and mires; places that are among the best known of all the attractions of beautiful Britain, yet which paradoxically have sides that are virtually unknown.

Cheddar, Wells and Glastonbury are visited annually by thousands who hope to assimilate in a day what loving hands took centuries to build, or what nature took tens of thousands of years to create. The moors around and between them are, on the other hand, among the least explored parts of the West Country, rich though they are in natural beauty, history, and legend. Of such contrasts is Somerset made.

Central Somerset, the area bounded roughly by the Mendip Hills on the north-east and by the River Parrett on the south-west, consists of two specially contrasted types of country: the dry Mendips rising abruptly to over 1,000 feet above sea level, and the completely flat moors that were once the bed of an inland sea, a world of pollarded willows and ruler-straight drainage ditches known locally as rhynes. Both uplands and fenlands still hold within themselves secrets of nature herself, and of man's evolution and earliest being. Fantastic though the publicly shown caves of Cheddar may be, others of at least equal wonder are known to be hidden in the Mendips while, though our knowledge of ancient man and his habitations has been fascinatingly enlarged by the discovery and excavation of the strange lake-villages near Glastonbury, those lush green pastures almost certainly hide other important clues to our remotest ancestry.

Of the two, perhaps the moors hold the greatest attraction for those who know Somerset well. Miles of long, lazily waving grasses and reeds stretch to an infinite pale blue horizon. Straight rhynes lined with the ubiquitous willows form a characteristic pattern of neatly-defined squares in a landscape without hedges. Seen from any eminence, they appear as a crisscross pattern of gleaming silver lines on a green patchwork quilt, dotted with the peacefully grazing cattle that outnumber people by dozens to one. The clank of milk churns is heard more than the roar of traffic. Here is utter tranquillity that insinuates itself into the soul. To those who know and love them, the moors are Somerset.

It is interesting to take a contoured map of this central region, and to colour in blue the land beneath the lowest contour line. Then the layout of the former islands and dry land emerges from the blue representing water, giving some idea of the area's probable appearance in the days when much of it was submerged. Long narrow fingers of elevated land, then peninsulas and off-shore islands, rise from the bed of what was a shallow lagoon, part sea, part marsh, part mere. Most prominent are the sharp Wedmore ridge, the narrower Polden Hills, and the isolated island masses including the conspicuous Brent Knoll and Glastonbury, also known as the legendary Avalon.

This damp region was a place of gentle ripples and marshy fringes, where fishing was the few inhabitants' livelihood. Sometimes, however, the placid waters took on a more threatening aspect, as high tides roared in from the Bristol Channel. Deep water channels enabled ships to penetrate as far inland as Avalon. These were well known to the Romans who sailed in to their lead mines on the Mendips, one of which is held to have been owned by Joseph of Arimathea, a wealthy Eastern merchant who was a close disciple – some indeed say, actually a relative – of Christ Himself. After the Crucifixion Joseph understandably returned, this time as a missionary, creating some of the greatest of the Glastonbury legends and building the tiny chapel from which grew one of the premier abbeys of England.

Neither the moors nor these former islands were always as peaceful as they are now, blessed havens from the modern world.

Introduction

Bloody deeds as well as holy ones have stained this soil. Here men fought bitterly against their own countrymen in a futile cause, and here the routed rebels of Sedgemoor were hanged and mutilated. Judicial murder has been committed in apparently smiling Somerset in the name of the law or of distorted religion by the ruthless Judge Jeffreys and by the Reformation despoilers who executed a frail and saintly abbot atop a Somerset hill before his own townspeople. The land that saw the first flicker of the Christian light in England lit by followers of its very Founder, saw good and holy men of that same religion hounded to ignominious death, and the glory that was the mighty Glastonbury Abbey desecrated and destroyed.

King Alfred in particular played an important part in the area's early history, a good king, a fine military strategist and a cultured man of learning who gave us one of our most important records of those far-off days, the Anglo-Saxon Chronicle. Naturally his deeds have been overlaid with unsubstantiated stories, though archaeology does have a delightful habit in these parts of sometimes unearthing concrete evidence that brings such figures a little nearer the light of modern understanding; the very recent discovery of parts of King Alfred's palace at Cheddar is but one example.

Glastonbury treasures the names of King Arthur and his Queen Guinevere, though sceptics doubt the truth of the story of the finding of their first burial place, and of their re-interment in the Abbey in the reigning king's presence. The recent spate of discoveries lends hope that this will some day be proved.

The story of this countryside of shivering reeds and now richly fertile fens goes even further back into historic twilight. The most primitive of people inhabited the marshy shores around Avalon, living in simple huts raised on platforms at the water's edge, thereby to discourage marauding enemies and wild animals. Their strange dwellings have been carefully excavated, adding much to our knowledge of our dimmest ancestors. If modern archaeology and historical science thus proves rather than disproves the story of ancient man, can we lightly discount those tales which have not yet been substantiated? Writers – usually not of Somerset extraction – like to dismiss the theory that St. Joseph of Arimathea really came here, but they are always confronted by one piece of tangible evidence: the Holy Thorn in spring flower while winter winds howl across the open moors. Though icicles literally hang by the wall, the Thorn still blossoms as the legend says, at Christmas.

Few counties include two such utterly different types of country virtually side by side as the central Somerset moors and the Mendip Hills. The world of light and open space where men lived among quivering osiers comes to within a couple of miles of caves where they inhabited a deep, dank underworld of bats and dripping walls, with beasts unknown to us as company. Skeletons of extraordinary age have been found at Cheddar and other places.

Cheddar cliffs, beneath which a strange world of astonishing beauty lies, tower to sheer 500-foot walls as though nature had sliced the hills apart with a giant axe, only about twenty minutes' walk from the moors' edge.

But what can or need be said of this eternal magnet to the tripper and the profiteer, when its underground mysteries have been lauded a thousand times, and illuminated with modern floodlighting for the benefit of dutifully attentive parties who will be gone tomorrow, convinced that they have "done" Cheddar? Cheddar, the real Cheddar, can never be exhausted as a subject, because its marvels are still inexhaustible. Those who visit the caves and stroll a few yards into the immediate vicinity no more see the whole Cheddar than passing visitors see a London which eternally surprises with fresh corners and new aspects those who have lived a lifetime there. Cheddar is not only an afternoon tour in sunshine; it is eerie dusk over towering black crags, misty morning silence broken only by cawing birds among the high natural pinnacles, dizzy perches on the brink of a sheer plunge to a road full of unreal toytown cars, dragonflies hovering around wild yellow irises, strawberry picking on mild quiet hills, the descent of peace in the warm evening when the last coaches have gone. All this and much, much more, is Cheddar.

One of the loveliest of all cathedral cities also lies cradled under the Mendips, as if the beauty of Wells were so precious that it must be sheltered from all but the gentlest winds. The most obvious and famous marvels of Wells are alone sufficient to draw people from the world's opposite ends. "This is the one place in England that is completely perfect. Yes, just perfect", an American said to me recently. A young Malaysian girl only the previous day had said: "It's so beautiful, I want to cry". If this peerless blend of medieval towers above immaculate lawns, ancient gateways, great old trees, and a romantic moated Palace can make people from the farthest East weep, and from farthest West want to live there after a mere glance, how much more can it give to those who stay long enough to see the less obvious sides of Wells? There is Wells at dusk, when old clocks chime across silent meadows where the last birds twitter; Wells in gentle West Country rain that only softens its beauty to a more delicate tone; Wells at Christmas; in snow; when Sunday bells toll. Yet it keeps abreast of the modern world, to the faint surprise of those who imagine that cathedral cities must be dull and staid. Golden Olympic rings let into the Market Square's pavement mark the exact long-jump distance that took a Wells girl to a world record in far-off Tokyo: even the paving stones tell a story, and it may be of today as well as of yesterday.

Similarly, Glastonbury's noble ruins are but a part of Avalon, though their beauty even in decay is reason enough for coming to Glastonbury. But how many go on, to climb the Tor, though this landmark dominates half the county? The views are breathtaking, even as far as the Welsh mountains and the sea, and the geographical picture of islands and marshlands of old can here be understood more clearly than from any textbook. The Abbey is Glastonbury's heart, but there are many other things to see, not all of them visible at a casual glance.

Cheddar, Wells and Glastonbury need to be lived with, or at least visited frequently at all times of year and in all weathers, and explored with a receptive mind for their messages of peace and wonder, before they surrender their inner selves. When they do, they are part of one's being for ever.

This volume, then, attempts to show, as well as the well-known Somerset, something of the other Somerset. It points out a few of the many contrasts, as sharp as the geographical differences between upland and moorland, open sky and underground caverns, of the interesting section of the county bounded approximately by the Mendips and the Parrett basin.

It does not pretend to be comprehensive, or that no activity and no industry has been overlooked. Nor is it a formal date-scattered history, though the past is inevitably woven into it, the past being the very soul of Somerset. Certainly it makes no attempt at completeness; many excellent guide-books already serve the county more than well. Instead, it takes a sometimes unashamedly personal glance at this land of legend, history, and beauty, spiced with memories from the near-past to the present while yet remembering that Somerset is by no means confined for its prosperity to milk churns, cider and cheeses.

Glastonbury
Saints and Sheepskin Boots

GLASTONBURY, the legendary Isle of Avalon, is the heart of central Somerset geographically, historically, and spiritually. Many other names have adorned it: Ynniswytryn (variously spelled), Mother of Saints, Secret of the Lord, Blessed Isle; from the Saxon came Glastonbury, or town of glass. Tennyson later wrote of "the island valley of Avilion, where falls not hail nor rain or any snow, nor ever wind blows loudly", not a strictly accurate description as anyone knowing West Country rain can testify. One winter it rained, rained, and continued raining for five weeks if youthful memory serves aright. Perhaps the elements were more amenable in Tennyson's day.

Glastonbury has been linked with the earliest Christian church as far back as the very boyhood of Christ. The tradition that He trod Somerset soil in boyhood is extremely ancient, which some understanding of the district's geography shows to be possible.

In Roman times much of what is now flat moorland was submerged beneath an arm of the sea, part salt water, part mere, part marsh; opinions differ as to the proportion of water to morass and mire, but certainly water in some form covered the greater part of this low-lying area. The ridges and hills were islands, of which the largest was Avalon. The sea has gone, though a stretch known as The Mere lingered as late as the 18th century, leaving the land as flat as the proverbial billiard table. In winter these moors may flood, though less often than 20 years ago; then the country regains something of its old appearance, enabling those who know the Somerset the tourists miss to understand better the background to the story of the coming of Christ.

It is revealing to approach Avalon from the moors on foot, which gives a surprisingly realistic idea of coming in slowly by boat towards a shore. Walking from, say, the Street side, the land rises from a sea of grass instead of water but the outline is recognisably island-like. Heady sea breezes blow off the Bristol Channel across the flat fields, refreshing and exhilarating. Approaching Avalon, the meadows merge into a very gentle rise, only noticeable to alert eyes, as though a beach shelved from the water's edge. Even the air changes; the bright moorland wind gives way to the warmth of a sheltered land, carrying distinctly off the "shore". The sensation is very like sailing into a protected harbour.

Ships could come this far inland at one time, from the Roman Empire of which Britain was part, following trade routes through the Mediterranean, round Cornwall, and into the Bristol Channel from which Somerset's shallow waters continued. The Mendip Hills were rich in the lead the Romans sought, and are still riddled with old lead mines. One, reputedly identifiable, was owned by Joseph of Arimathea, a well-to-do merchant said to have been related to the young Christ, as an uncle of His Mother. Such a man would naturally have visited his interests in Britain, the tin of Cornwall and the lead of Somerset, via the usual route up the Bristol Channel. As today a man of property might occasionally take a favourite relative on a journey to broaden the lad's education, so Joseph, tradition says, brought the boy at least once to Britain, showing Him something of the great Empire. Thus Somerset people believe He may have set foot on their shores. Undeniably His life between the ages of 12 and 30 is unrecorded, during which He was presumably prepared for the coming ministry; what better preparation than meeting all manner of people in other lands with His travelling uncle?

If Joseph did bring Jesus to England, it must have been where his business took him, to the West Country. A tale of superstitious country folk? Not only they; Blake, one of the greatest religious thinkers, pondered the story seriously and reverently, putting his thoughts into his Glastonbury Hymn, better known as "Jerusalem":

> And did those feet in ancient time
> Walk upon England's mountains green?

Did those feet, Blake wonders, tread the 1,000 foot heights of Mendip where His uncle had his trade?

> And was the holy Lamb of God
> On England's pleasant pastures seen?

Did the youth's penetrating eyes rest on Avalon's pastures?

> And did the countenance divine
> Shine forth upon our clouded hills?

Was it the cloud-attracting isolated Glastonbury Tor the poet meant, the greatest landmark to ships sailing towards Somerset? And was "England's green and pleasant land" this greenest and pleasantest of counties? Blake, scholars suggest, was a seer and visionary rather than deeply learned in every turn of localised history. At the very least, however, he put into inspired words thoughts which people can take up, think and read further on, and draw what conclusions they will.

Joseph of Arimathea is the kingpin of the Glastonbury legends, builder of the first church and bringer of the Holy Thorn. After the Crucifixion he was one of the first to obey the command "go ye into all the world and preach the Gospel". Instinctively he must have set course for the land where he had traded, where he would be received favourably. To Avalon he therefore came, with eleven companions, perhaps forming a band of twelve in remembrance of the twelve of the Upper Room; we can only surmise that the number had some significance.

Tradition says that Joseph carried the Chalice of the Last Supper, others say he bore two cruets containing blood and sweat of the Crucifixion. Old coats of arms show two crossed shoots of the Holy Thorn flanked by the cruets, against falling drops of blood.

Gently Joseph's craft glided in, her passengers weary from the long voyage; Weary-all Hill is that spot's name even now. Landing, he thrust his stout thorn staff into the fertile earth, which forthwith rooted to become a strong young tree. This was no ordinary thorn; it blossomed at Christmas as well as in spring. It has even been speculated that the staff itself was a special one. According to eastern tradition a man's staff was passed to his eldest son or nearest male relative in a deathbed ceremony. Joseph as the nearest relative may possibly, then, have carried Our Lord's own staff.

The Holy Thorn springing from Joseph's staff survived for centuries until a Puritan fanatic in anti-Rome zeal resolved to destroy this symbol of the old faith. He succeeded in hacking off one of the two massive branches; in attacking the second, we are told, he met his retribution when a great splinter flying into his eye killed him. Another version holds that in chopping at the stubborn old wood he cut off his own foot.

The tree lingered about thirty years before dying, during which time young thorns were reared from it. They and their offspring grow around Glastonbury still, evidence of a tale that would otherwise be without visible foundation. One grows in the Abbey ruins, and a splendid specimen in St. John's churchyard; others are said to exist in private gardens. They do flower at Christmas. Winter can be severe when winds howling across unbroken moors slash Avalon, but the Holy Thorns faithfully blossom; I remember as a child seeing this spring-like blossom as usual during the worst winter for decades, shaking in an icy wind under leaden skies. Nor is even the second spring flowering quite normal; recently I noticed ancient thorns near the Abbey as heavy with blossom as with white snow, but the Holy Thorn was nearly finished. It seems to flower a couple of weeks earlier in May.

During 1951, a young thorn was planted on the slopes of Wearyall Hill on what is believed to be the site of the original tree, marking the Festival of Britain year.

Offshoots of the Holy Thorns have been planted in many places, from St. Andrew's in Scotland to a Surrey churchyard, some of which survived. One offshoot was sent to the United States for planting beside the grave of President Wilson. But there is one strange fact about such plantings in general; for two years they appear to flourish, and then inexplicably die. With a few exceptions, they just do not like ground outside Glastonbury. Why? Our ancestors undoubtedly would have woven magical meanings into this proven fact; we can but note it with interest and wonder. Another interesting point: if gardeners try to raise them from the actual berry, the result is an ordinary thorn, that does not flower at Christmas.

Botanists identify the Thorn as Crataegus Praecox, a Levantine thorn, which bears out the story of its coming from the east. It can be budded but not struck. Charles I among others noted that it confounded the Pope by blooming on old Christmas Day rather than the new; the blossom is noticeably at its best then.

A favourite local folksong carries the theme of a tree, an interminable affair on the lines of Old Macdonald's Farm which, after a day at the seaside, a van-load of tireless passengers could stretch most of the drive from Burnham to Street. A typical verse goes something like:

> Now on this branch there was a twig
> The prettiest twig you ever did see.
> And the twig was on the branch,
> And the branch was on the bough,
> And the bough was on the trunk,
> And the trunk was on the tree,
> And the tree was in the wood,
> And the wood was in the West Country.
> And the green leaves grew all round, around, around,
> And the green leaves grew all round.

Did we sing of a special tree, the tree? Probably, for the Thorn was the heart of Glastonbury. The original did grow in, or rather near, a wood; once I was shown the supposed site not far from the distinctive square shaped wood on Weary-all Hill, just above what would have been the seashore.

Joseph of Arimathea and his companions erected a tiny wattle church, one of the first if not the very first in England. For centuries it was revered and preserved as the work of Christ's own followers, successive monasteries incorporating this Vetusta Ecclesia. It survived an incredible 1,100 years; William of Malmesbury in 1143 said: "It is a little old place, but it is so holy". Near the present ruined Chapel of St. Mary, locally called St. Joseph's, supposedly on the same site, stands a massive cross of unadorned wood, "the symbol of our faith". This gift of Queen Elizabeth II "marks a Christian sanctuary so ancient that only legend can record its origin". So in our own time the first church on what has been called the holiest ground in England is commemorated through our reigning Queen.

In 1184 the entire earlier Abbey including the Vetusta Ecclesia was destroyed by fire. Recent excavations have unearthed hitherto unknown fragments; buried for centuries, masonry has been recovered still blackened by flame and smoke. Some pieces are untouched, and of a singular beauty.

The new church, whose ruins we now visit, must have been one of the most splendid ever to rise from the ashes of another. It became the premier abbey of England, the burial place of kings, and attracted numberless pilgrims to where the light of their faith was first kindled. One of the stations at which they paused survives on an ancient wall, the simple inscription "Jesus Maria".

Only seven feet shorter than Ely Cathedral, the great church was unusual in that the Lady Chapel – locally St. Joseph's – was at the

Glastonbury Abbey Ruins - The nave and choir.

west end instead of the east, continuing the tradition that this was the site of the wattle church. This chapel, the most beautiful and complete part of the ruins, has ornate turrets, fine window detail, and a remarkably carved north doorway. In the crypt an altar has been built, allowing occasional services to be held as close as possible to where the first prayers were offered at Glastonbury. To gain an impression of the overall layout at Glastonbury, Durham Cathedral makes a useful comparison. Built within a few years of Glastonbury, it likewise has a Lady Chapel at the west end instead of the east, connected to the nave by a rather similar "Galilee", and was of the same Benedictine Order.

The noble ruins indicate the majestic Abbey's size, but we can only visualise the splendour within. The costly gifts of exalted pilgrims continually enriched its shrines, chapels, and priceless library. There was a wonderful mechanical clock, counterpart of that at Wells, where smiths struck the hours on bells. The church was extended until the very eve of the Reformation.

Abbots lived apart in princely style, exercising spiritual and judicial authority and entertaining the highest in the land. Edward I

The Abbot's Kitchen, Glastonbury Abbey.

and Queen Eleanor spent Holy Week here in 1278; in 1494 Henry VII was given a specially built apartment, added to a home which must have shown little of monastic poverty and humility. The Abbots' Kitchen, still intact, has four huge corner fireplaces whose flues meet a great central lantern; if this was but the kitchen, how splendid must have been the house. On Church business Abbots travelled widely for their day: thus Abbot Forde set a mystery over 100 miles away which historians cannot explain – did he die, or was he murdered? Bishops of Rochester, like most Church dignitaries, held property throughout their dioceses, including a palace at Bromley in Kent. There one day in 1261 Abbot Forde of Glastonbury stayed, and there he died. According to certain accounts he was killed at Bromley during a journey "to defend the rights of his church", which some interpret as murder. Earlier and presumably more reliable versions merely state that Forde died suddenly, of what cause we are not told, but ghoulish humanity obstinately prefers an ecclesiastical who-dun-it. Whatever the truth, at least one Abbot before the last left Glastonbury, not to return alive.

The Abbey parks included vegetable gardens, and a vineyard on Weary-all Hill. It has been said that cultivation of the vine is not practicable in our climate, but Somerset is one of the few quarters where grape growing has met with some success. Southern Britain had many vineyards in the Middle Ages, and in recent years the idea of reviving English wines has suddenly flowered, notably at Beaulieu in Hampshire.

Three kings were buried in the Abbey: Edmund the Doer of Great Deeds, Edmund Ironside, and Edgar the Giver of Peace, but above all hangs the spirit of King Arthur, the half legendary soldier-hero. In 1191 his grave was reputedly discovered in an ancient cemetery outside the abbey, marked by two obelisks. Under the heavy gravestone was a leaden cross marked "Hic jacet sepultur inclitus Rex Arthuris in insula Avalonia ..." When the grave was opened, they say, Queen Guinevere's golden hair was seen for an instant, vanishing into dust at the touch of air. Romantic fiction? In the 20th century came a discovery of similar nature, fully documented: during excavations of the unique moorland lake-villages, felled trees were unearthed, their chippings white and freshly cut, which immediately turned grey; autumn and summer leaves were found, in perfect colour, which became colourless within minutes. Perhaps something similar applied to Guinevere, for the two instances are not disimilar and occurred only a few miles apart.

A black marble shrine was prepared, where in 1278 they were reinterred before the High Altar in the presence of Edward I and Queen Eleanor. The shrine's base was found in 1934 and is indicated by stone surrounds. The original grave has been identified in the old cemetery. Some still question the story, but would a reigning monarch have lent his patronage to the ceremonious re-burial of anyone of

> SITE OF KING ARTHUR'S TOMB.
> IN THE YEAR 1191 THE BODIES OF
> KING ARTHUR AND HIS QUEEN WERE
> SAID TO HAVE BEEN FOUND ON THE
> SOUTH SIDE OF THE LADY CHAPEL.
> ON 19TH APRIL 1278 THEIR REMAINS WERE
> REMOVED IN THE PRESENCE OF
> KING EDWARD I AND QUEEN ELEANOR
> TO A BLACK MARBLE TOMB ON THIS SITE.
> THIS TOMB SURVIVED UNTIL THE
> DISSOLUTION OF THE ABBEY IN 1539

King Arthur's grave in the choir of Glastonbury Abbey.

lesser stature? Despite all this, doubt is still cast on the whole subject of Arthur and Avalon, and probably always will be. Only the discovery of authentic records of contemporary date could truly settle the old question, a rather unlikely possibility now. Nevertheless, the story lingers, and books constantly appear offering anything from complete disbelief to attempted proof, in forms from scholarly treatises to American Arthuriana. Whatever the truth, the subject never fails to exercise people's minds and pens.

On the road to Street, still locally called The Causeway, is Pomparles Bridge, more accurately Pons Parlous or Pons Perilis. The Roman route across these fens lay closely parallel, founded on timber overlaid with brushwood and stones. Here, from an earlier Pons Perilis, was Arthur's sword Excalibur flung into the lake. Twice the knight instructed to destroy the dying king's sword felt unable to throw away such a treasure. The third time he resolutely flung it far into the mere. A white-clad arm, as Tennyson tells, rose to catch Excalibur, "brandished him three times, and drew him under in the mere". Does it lie somewhere here? If so the proven preservative property of peat must keep it safely to itself.

Arthur and the saints brought many pilgrims, for whom accommodation was necessary. The exalted were regally entertained at the Abbey, the moderately affluent at the Pilgrim's Inn; lesser hostelries took those who came in humble piety without ostentation. The chapel on Glastonbury Tor was an additional pilgrim's goal. It is said that sinners were sometimes ordered as penance to climb the steep hill with hardened peas in their shoes, making reparation in Mass at the summit.

Inevitably greedy eyes turned at the Reformation to Glastonbury's riches. Richard Whiting, its last Abbot, feeling the approach of tragedy, hid the most precious plate and treasure. He did it well; it has never apparently been found, for the secret died with Whiting on the gallows. No wonder the despoiler felt robbed of such prey: silver plate, golden chalices, jewelled candlesticks, ivory crucifixes, lavish hangings; the silver plate alone is said to have exceeded 11,000 ounces.

Abbot Whiting, accused of stealing this treasure, was convicted of treason in a travesty of a trial. Sad onlookers, scarcely believing that a wise and goodly ruler was to die a traitor's death, saw him and other monks dragged, stripped of their habits, through the town towards the Tor, followed by the executioner's cart with its dreadful paraphernalia. On the summit they were hanged, drawn and quartered, within sight of the Abbey at the height of its splendour, in its very last hours.

The church was destroyed and the ruins plundered for building materials. Now the remains are protected and prevented from further crumbling by ingenious replacement of vital stone-work, discreetly done. The piers of the crossing give some idea of the church's height, and the arches' decoration a glimpse of its elaboration. St. Joseph's Chapel is in reality as big as many a parish church, yet looks insignificant against the entire Abbey. Such is the glory that is gone.

Though Glastonbury, like many other suppressed monasteries, became a free quarry for local builders, as is evident from many a local stone wall today, later generations have on occasion plundered the ruins with more reverent intent. Thus did James Austin, a 19th-century owner of the ruins, by whose gift a beautiful carved stone from one of the great abbey doorways was removed to the London parish of Deptford in 1882. There it was incorporated into the fabric of a church where visible beauty was to play a more than merely decorative purpose, one built with a theatrically raked floor ensuring that all worshippers should see the priest's hands – a church specifically for the deaf and dumb.

Thousands come sightseeing to the place that is so lovely in decay, and find something that is not in their guide-books: perfect tranquillity that can, if you let it, enter the very soul. What is it about this roofless ruin that touches people like a tangible thing? Perhaps the phrase: "the peace that passeth all understanding" best describes it. Even more is this peace given by Glastonbury to those who know it when the tourists have gone; November drizzle only softens the creamy-grey stones, earliest spring frames them in palest green lace, and dusk adds gentleness to bare walls instead of the gruesomeness of the Victorian "romantic" ruin.

Rather strangely, dusk does not appear to invite the ghosts one would expect of such a place. I cannot recall having either my juvenile or my present hair raised by tales of a beheaded abbot walking, not even a mere monk. In such a legend-soaked ruin a ghost would seem an almost compulsory resident. Perhaps there was enough of truth to make an additional ghost unnecessary in attracting visitors and their purses. It is a minor point in favour of the legends.

Every tourist sees the Abbey, but fewer make the lengthy walk to the Tor. The climb is stiff, especially on the sharp middle ridge when the moorland breeze bangs the climber as if trying to sweep him or her off its property. Then, as one regular climber always remarked, one feels obliged to "hang onto a blade of grass".

The cows which regard the Tor as their domain may vie with the wind in discouraging nervous walkers; when in calf – which seems to be about once a week – they gallop down territory we humans only crawl up. "Therr bain't no harm in they", countrymen insist, but have never cured my cow-complex, the result of being snatched from the path of a stampeding herd on Weary-all Hill.

Giants, winds and cows negotiated, the views are breathtaking, embracing a complete circle. The moors that were the sea bed stretch to the Channel on the far horizon, where the sea sometimes shines silver, with the island of Steep Holme farther out, and perhaps even the south Welsh mountains. Such clarity usually means approaching rain. In another direction Wells Cathedral dreams under the Mendips, a jewel in an emerald setting. The whole world is at one's feet. The moorland dykes, locally called rhynes, shine as a silver network on a green patchwork quilt, formal and symmetrical but magical.

The chapel on the Tor has vanished, leaving only its tower as the most prominent landmark in Somerset, centrepiece of the entire area. On the tower's wall a plaque records that the chapel was "rebuilt after

St. Michael's Church Tower on Glastonbury Tor.

an earthquake about 1300 A.D. This tower was added about 1360 A.D., and is all that now remains".

Orchards have traditionally surrounded the lower Tor, where breezes and sun bless the crops; not for nothing was this called Apple Isle. There are eating apples as well as the ubiquitous cider or "scrumpy" apples. Owners sometimes leave large boxes of windfalls and other unwanted fruit outside, temptingly labelled: "Please help yourself".

Under the Tor is Chalice Well, where legend says Joseph of Arimathea hid the holy Chalice. Its red-brown waters, found to have curative properties, made the town a short-lived spa in the 18th century. The stream from it rushes alongside the lane to the Tor.

Running downwards from the Tor, the High Street is given an attraction it might otherwise lack by its steep slant. Here is the ancient Tribunal where Abbots dealt temporal rule. After the Dissolution it was a house and a school, its interior consequently defaced. On most archaeological sites all wood has disappeared, but the waterlogged Somerset peat has preserved such things as iron implements with wooden handles, apparently almost new. There is even a strange object believed to be a small cake mixed with honey, coloured beads, a pin remarkably like a modern safety pin, and the Glastonbury Bowl of beautiful yellowish grey-green showing a raised knob decoration. One could devote hours to examining the craftsmanship of these peoples of the waters. Even today water is near the surface, seeping through excavations, much as is seen in the lower lying areas of Holland when digging downwards.

St. John's Church dominates the High Street with its lofty tower; tower and chancel were built by the abbey, the rest by the parish, an ingenious spreading of the financial burden. The north transept window records the Arimathea legends, showing St. Joseph in rich purple. The lower lights show him protesting at Christ's condemnation, at the entombment, landing at Glastonbury with the two sacred cruets while a sailing ship rides in the background, and planting his staff. On the transept wall hangs an ancient pall made from a cope worn by the martyred Abbot Whiting. In the chancel is kept a crucifix reputedly owned by, of all people, Judge Jeffreys, whose Bloody Assize sent so many to the gallows on trumpery charges. If ever the cross was worn hypocritically, it was this.

The churchyard has the biggest Holy Thorn generally visible, a tangled mass of foliage. "Aw arr, 'ee had a wonderful spread o' blossom last Christmas" a local character confirmed when I asked lately whether it was as good as ever.

St. Benignus, or Benedict, stands near the merging of land and former mere. Local people will point out floodmarks where the water in flood years attempted to reclaim its own. For years a stone is said to have recorded the great 1606 inundation when the sea swept back to its old bed. Perhaps we should not say it is gone but is only, in

Somerset parlance, "biding its time". The threat of flooding has one beneficial effect: it prevents new towns growing on the moors, or new estates below existing towns.

Glastonbury might easily appear to be all churches and churchmen, pilgrims and saints. In fact, lightheartedness is no more unknown than in any country town. In its railway days there were happy Sunday School treats to Burnham-on-Sea by special steam trains behind veteran locomotives, which were fed from thick dangling hoses before rumbling off on the crawl to the sea, a bedlam of singing youngsters. After this, the station went to sleep again until noon. There were three trains daily, morning, noon, and evening, connecting with other old puffers for Wells or Evercreech (Everscreech to the young). The returning special was met by assorted conveyances; my personal favourite was the small trailer attached to vans for delivering sheep and pigs, preferring to stand in a trailer smelling of pig than to sit on a respectable seat.

The railway was brought here by the enterprising and public-spirited Clarks, whose works outings were exhausting affairs. A poster of 1885 advertises a trip to Plymouth at the unholy hour of 5:30 a.m., a five-hour journey, returning around 1 a.m. next morning. And then they had to go on to Street. The factory band went to enliven the party, presumably blowing all the way back as well. All this for 4s. 3d. – return!

With such thoughts I wandered onto the now deserted platforms one day, seeing in the mind's eye the cheerful activity of steam trains and cattle trucks, clanking shunting, and a hand-operated level crossing. From a cottage beside the overgrown tracks a ruddy-faced Zummerzet type appeared, all anxiety and concern. "Be 'ee waiting for Lunnon train, Miss?" he enquired. "The last one 'ee went five yurr ago. Therr bain't been no trains since". Five years being a long wait even by rural standards, I retraced my sentimental steps, passing the infants' school outside which was a poster reading "You've seen My Fair Lady, you've seen The Sound of Music. But you've seen nothing until you've been to our pantomime Snow White and the Seven Dwarfs". It must have been a stupendous production.

Childish railway pleasures included the so-called Tin Bridge. This contraption rises to a sudden hump, fenced with corrugated iron instead of wood, hence its name. A good bus driver was one who put his foot down on the accelerator when approaching the Tin Bridge and shot his passengers over a few seconds ahead of their tummies. Modern drivers by these standards have deteriorated; they seem not to drive with the same abandon.

In my childhood two amusement companies merged on the same ground, including steam driven roundabouts; Mother and I used to sit on Weary-all Hill watching for the first smoke from the little round chimneys on their roofs, for getting up steam meant opening time. The centrepiece was the steam-chariots, great red-lined golden gondolas with elaborately carved curving ends, revolving switchback-wise to the smell of steam and the sound of a genuine steam organ of remarkable depth and richness of tone. A young cousin once had four rides in succession by screaming and clinging like a leech whenever it stopped, forcing his father to pay for another round as the gondolas moved off again. "I'll give thee a leathering" was his favourite threat; he carried it out that time. There were also steam-yachts like huge boat-swings, and terrifying wire cages swinging ever higher until they swung right over the bar, the Moonrocket, and, of course, roundabout horses galloping to authentic fairground organs. This may all read like great-grandma's day out, but in fact many of these marvellous examples of the fairground builders' ornate art, built around 1900, exist today in working order, regularly travelling the country to such events as the Bath and West Show.

The town that saw the first Christian light, and has ever since been centred round the famous Abbey marking the site of that first humble church, no more lets itself become sanctimoniously staid than does the average town or village. Fairs, fetes and carnivals are as beloved of Glastonians as of all country people.

There is apparently little of intrusive modernity or industry on Glastonbury's surface, yet many of the visitors who arrive in spring or autumn chill may be wearing the most important part of its contemporary economy on their own feet: boots trademarked Morlands. Such footwear once took Glastonbury's name close to the top of the world, for Morland's boots were worn by the conquerors of Everest, not for climbing but for the equally important purpose of warming the party's feet when resting in their bivouacs.

Somerset sheep and wool meant the presence of tanners and fellmongers. In 1822 one of these, Arthur Clothier, went into partnership with a fellow Quaker, Cyrus Clark, already an astute businessman at 21. When the partnership foundered, Clark continued rugmaking alone, engaging his 17-year-old brother James as an apprentice. That enterprising lad began experimenting with rejected skins in warmly lined slippers, and then with fleecy socks worn inside shoes. The expanding business later acquired the disused tannery at Northover where the present factory stands, and the Clarks with another Quaker, John Morland, formed the partnership which made the firm a separate entity from Clark's shoes of Street.

The advent of the motor car was the turning point, when the first motorists discovered that the horseless carriage had its discomforts. Huddled in rugs they tasted the first shivering fruits of the new age. Morlands astutely cashed in with sheepskin rugs, followed by footmuffs into which they later inserted an ingenious hot-water-bottle holder. The closed car ended the demand for footmuffs, but Morland's were ready to pursue new trails in the cause of warm feet. Bedroom slippers followed, for many years called Glastonburys, hard soled slippers for more demanding wear, and overshoes of reversed sheepskin; not unlike clumsy Wellingtons, these paved the way towards the present boot.

Lean times came with the Depression, when the only hard working department was Morland's Unemployed, whose mission was to score goals against football teams from other affected factories. What did the directors do while their workers played football and collected the dole? Cut their own salaries, and planned for expansion. The Depression, they deduced, must in the natural order of things precede a boom. During the enforced lull they embarked on apparently reckless building programmes, which paid off handsomely; when the boom came, they were prepared.

The present warm-lined leather boot was finalised, now considered among the best footwear in the world. A Morland's price tag may have appeared extravagant, but a glance into the complicated processing reverses such an impression. The skins were pulled wet through rollers whose teeth remove matter entangled in the wool, followed by intensive further cleaning to remove all trace of fat. They were then tanned or bleached according to their destinations as slipper linings, rugs, or heavier duty work. On great frames they were stretched to dry, over 1,100 skins at once, then softened and sorted and cleaned yet again. All lanolin was removed, sold as a separate product, and the skins dyed to any colour fashion cared to dictate, or left white for linings. 100,000 skins were stored together, for use in the factory or for sale. The actual footwear-making was itself long and skilled, using expert craftsmen as well as machines. Soles and uppers fixed, the product went for a final "beauty treatment" and checking. Morland's shoes and boots are cheap at the price.

John Morland himself died in harness at the great age of 96; another leading light combined a life devoted to sheepskins with literary activity, writing a standard book on that most unsheep-like creature the dragon. Another married a daughter of General Smuts. I recall passing with Mother a tall, soldierly gentleman in country squire plus-fours, who bid we strangers a courtly "Good morning". "Do 'ee know where 'ee be?" a relative asked. "'ee be General Smuts". If courtesy to a passing villager is typical of greatness, then Smuts deserved that description.

That overworked word where Somerset is concerned, contrast, applies very much to Glastonbury. The premier seat of English Christianity from its birth, it saw that seat destroyed and its abbot murdered in the name of the law. It rises from land as flat as a Dutch polder to the most prominent landmark in Somerset. On the surface it still revolves around its abbey, yet its prosperity comes from an industry which has taken its name to the icy slopes of Everest.

Street

Philanthropists and Factories

STREET is Clarks: Clarks is Street. The famous shoe factory and the town are virtually one unit created by one family, who combined an insistence on the best workmanship with, for their age, a quite extraordinary regard for their workers' welfare.

The Clarks were Quakers, a sect strongly represented around the Polden Hills, who saw that a factory town need not mean the poverty and dinginess of the northern mill towns which gave industry such a bad reputation. A good worker, they reasoned with business sense as well as Nonconformist Christianity, is a contented, well-housed individual labouring in humane conditions, with proper recreation to balance the working day. Thus in their wisdom and humanity the Clarks began in this former hamlet a small town existing by and through the factory under an enlightened ownership. Education, social life, welfare, creative leisure, healthy sport and adequate housing as well as a congenial workaday environment, were fostered from the start by these Quaker philanthropists.

1825 is the generally accepted year of the company's birth and with it the birth of modern Street, when Cyrus Clark set up in business on his own. His brother became his apprentice as a lad, and soon began experimenting in slipper-making with castoff skins from what was then chiefly a rug-making concern. So far the stories of Morlands and Clarks run a common course; Morlands, as has been seen in the previous chapter, eventually became a separate unit concentrating on sheepskins while the Clarks developed the shoe business at Street.

Much of the early shoe-making was done by outworkers in their own cottages; older Street residents vividly recall working by hand on fine leather.

The first machines brought the bulk of the work within the factory itself, a unification prompted both on business and humanitarian grounds; many of the outworkers' masters drank heavily for days after collecting their cash, while their young apprentices stood idle, being then forced to labour day and night to catch up in time for the next delivery. Thus emerged the parallel aims of a prospering business and the welfare of the village. Being of strong Quaker temperance views, the employers finally solved the drink problem by purchasing the inn opposite the factory purely to kill off its licence.

In very early days the "Tor" trademark – the lonely church tower on Glastonbury Tor with part of its summit – came to represent the best workmanship on the best leather. It is still used; when we buy shoes bearing this symbol we purchase the descendants of those made under the identical trademark over a century ago.

During World War II one huge workroom was taken over by the Government for the war effort; everyone seemed to be aware that something known vaguely as munitions was being turned out, but remembering that Street reputedly possessed only one air-raid shelter, residents maintained a commendable curtain of ignorance with strangers.

There was only one serious incident. One night armed commandos descended on the factory, and were met by the night shift with laudable bravery. Though their weapons ran to no more than fists and broomsticks, they tackled the invading parachutists and proudly marched them to the Home Guard room – only to discover that the whole raid was a military exercise.

Rationing challenged the factory's ingenuity; when rubber became scarce, hinged wooden soles were tried, and prototypes were issued to workers and their offspring for testing in actual wear, to the jealousy of the have-nots who, being unconnected with Clarks, lost this pearl so beloved of the English, something for nothing.

Street had its nasty moments when aircraft, chased from Bristol with bombs undropped, tended to spray them at random over the moors to speed their escape. From here people saw Bristol burning, though it lay nearly two hours' bus ride away beyond the Mendips, a huge ugly red glow on the horizon like the Fire of London. When a tradesman went next day to deliver goods the address had disappeared, and most of the surrounding area with it. Thenceforth, whenever the siren sounded meaning aircraft on the run loaded with excess bombs, he drove his van out onto the moors, feeling somehow safer in that wide, dark, lonely wilderness of meadows and water than in the confines of a cottage.

The fallen of both wars are commemorated in a little chamber under the creeper-clad factory clock tower. On one side is carved a girl at a sewing machine, on the other a young man in a leather apron with heavier machinery. The plaque naming the fallen is surmounted by the Tor symbol in gold on a green base. This chamber is almost chapel-like, quite unlike the usual standardised obelisk.

Clarks phenomenal growth since the war, exhausting most available local labour, has now necessitated opening new works in a dozen other West Country towns, but Street remains the headquarters, as by right it should.

Approaching Street from Glastonbury, visitors are agreeably surprised: could this picture of massive trees shading sloping lawns on both sides of the road be the main street of a factory town? Immaculate surrounding gardens no more tally with the subconscious concept of grimly functional industrial buildings does the clock tower which, not typically Victorian Gothic, faintly familiar air to the well travelled; it is in fact based on that of Thun cathedral in Switzerland.

Virtually everything for the public benefit in Street was of Clarks' doing, including neat attractive homes for their workers. These terraces have a certain architectural interest, broken by archways and gables. Wilfrid Road, near the factory, is considered a classic example, in the "arts and crafts" manner beloved of the later 19th century, of good factory housing. They encouraged thrift by opening a savings bank, and built the fine social centre, Crispin Hall; Crispin is the shoemakers' saint.

A reliable outlet for their products being vital, Clarks' influence brought the railway to nearby Glastonbury, serving the area for many years. The swimming pool was the personal gift to Street of a Clark lady. Surrounded by lawns and trees, it was a godsend to the local women who were previously discouraged from bathing because the men and boys persistently swam in the altogether, effectively excluding petticoat interference.

Street's schools have high standards – Clark's influence again. Strode School was specially opened to allow very young employees to continue their education one day a week while working the other four in the factory. From it has developed in recent years a full and very up-to-date complex, including a tertiary college and the Strode Theatre. In my own Elmhurst days we wore scarlet black-braided blazers in summer, with black pocket crests, and pale green dresses trimmed in fawn, much more interesting than the cities' unadventurous navy blue. So much for the country bumpkin's schooling.

The old Board School is a prominent feature of the middle High Street. My only outstanding memory is of fighting the form bully on the floor for a bent pen-nib, collecting a scar that lasted well beyond my 21st birthday; and I lost the nib. This was the culmination of long enduring his gibes at my habit of carrying every valued possession around in an ancient red cotton bag. "Do thee carry thicky brains around in thicky bag?" the bully was wont to yell from his bicycle.

Millfield, at the opposite extreme, is accepted as one of the most expensive British schools. It began in 1935 as a private establishment on a modest scale, but has expanded vastly lately and is still growing. It specially encourages promising athletes and sportsmen, and former pupils have subsquently entered the record books of several major sports at international level; they include Mary Bignal-Rand, Somerset's Olympic "Golden Girl".

As a town, Street is bright and bustling, centred on the wide main street which is clean to the point of bareness compared with the beautiful greenery near the factory. Renewing acquaintanceship recently, I found that it had a somehow more cheerfully modern look than previously. The shop window displays seemed brighter, and in general Street had managed to become a contemporary shopping centre without losing its identity. New stores had arrived, and a few smaller supermarkets, but they blended into the High Street without destroying its alignment. Some familiar businesses remained, including some which have traded under the same names since about the 1880s, though other trades of character had inevitably disappeared; among these was the hefty butcher who habitually wielded his bloodstained hatchet to hearty hymn tunes, usually "Onward Christian Soldiers".

Though Street has advanced greatly as a shopping and community centre during the last few years, it has happily not lost the country town atmosphere; women gossiping on pavements talk of rural pursuits in Somerset accents. It has changed, and yet not really changed. Street is recognisably Street; the modernisation in evidence in the principal shopping street consists of improvements to existing properties instead of a soulless tearing apart to appease the god of concrete towers and glass boxes.

Historically the town is linked with Glastonbury, to which it was joined at one time by the precursor of The Causeway. It shared in the visit in 1278 of Edward I and Queen Eleanor, when they spent Holy

Clark's shoe factory in Street.

Week and Easter at Glastonbury in a blaze of regal pomp and ceremony belying the sackcloth and ashes concept of Lent. The Abbot, however, drew the line at His Majesty's proposal to hold assizes there, infringing the Abbey's jurisdiction over the neighbourhood, for Glastonbury's rulers were powerful enough to dictate even to a king. Seeing some justice in the claim, the king held his assizes at nearby Street instead, though the whereabouts seem to be uncertain now.

The parish church is an ancient one, standing near where the last meadows joined the old salt marshes and meres. One of its incumbents was the Rev. Walter Raleigh, a nephew of Sir Walter, a staunch Royalist during the Civil War, the conflict that raged so bitterly in Somerset. Taking part in one of the war's many local skirmishes, the reverend gentleman was captured by the other side and duly hanged. The Friends' Meeting House beside the factory, a modest but classic little structure, reminds us that all that is best here came from the Quaker influence.

One of the seemingly unlikeliest events in Street's history had its origin on the other side of England at Colchester, where at exactly 9.19 a.m. on April 22nd 1884, Britain's most destructive earthquake of recent centuries tore churches and public buildings apart, wrecked villages for miles around, completely destroyed one historic church, littered peaceful quaysides with tiles and wreckage suggestive of the blitz of sixty years later, and left large swathes of East Anglia in utterly un-English after-quake confusion. From Scotland to the Isle of Wight sympathetic tremors caused damage that is curiously little remembered now, but Street is believed to be the farthest point west at which the tremor was recorded, despite the shelter of the intervening Mendips. As in London and elsewhere, the shock was most pronounced on upper floors; the national press thus recorded how a Street invalid was rocked in her bed, a sensation certain neighbours found difficult to accept until, many hours later, news of Britain's least known disaster reached Somerset from London.

Though Street is economically bound closely to the shoe factory, it is also a country place whose other main calling is agriculture. The outer edges of the town merge into the pastures of the Polden Hills and the moorland meadows, where graze the dairy cattle that are Somerset's lifeblood.

"Oi've come up from Zummerzet, where the zider apples grow" could well describe a visitor from the outer parts of Street, for the town is flanked by cider-apple orchards. On the gentle slopes they catch the sun, and the breezes blowing across the wide moors from the sea. They are quite unlike ordinary apple trees, low, stumpy, gnarled and thickset, and are covered in a good season with the little round apples of brilliantly shining scarlet, rather like clusters of Christmas tree decorations. An old fashioned cider press, as opposed to a formal factory, is worth sniffing; the scent itself is almost intoxicating, if one is lucky enough to find one of the few small private presses surviving today. Cider in bulk is made as a commercial proposition on a fairly big scale, particularly around the Shepton Mallet district, but the apples themselves continue to be grown widely in the county, not least near Street and the Polden villages.

As well as the bottled variety, cider is offered in shamelessly tourist-attracting containers inscribed: "Oi've come up from Zurnmerzet", to attract the eyes of tourists to such popular haunts as Cheddar and Wookey Hole. In Somerset inns cider is naturally one of the favourite brews, its effects as heady as much stiffer hard drinks if quaffed to excess; closing time in a licensed establishment within the tourist area of Somerset can be very interesting, when those who have sampled cider in large quantities emerge full of song and bonhomie, to discover that cider affects the legs as well as the brain.

Old fashioned scrumpy, the hard farmhouse brew as opposed to factory cider, has been imbibed for some curious reasons in the past. One of the strangest excuses, though alleged to be perfectly genuine, was the fumes of a sewage works near Wells; until modernisation of the plant made the excuse obsolete, men employed there regularly consumed large amounts of scrumpy in the course of the working week; the smell of cider was considered effective in preventing a worker being overcome by more noxious fumes. Only in the 1970s was this long standing custom defeated – by mechanisation costing half a million pounds.

Stone quarrying was traditionally an important pursuit above Street towards the Polden Hills. Most older houses are of the distinctive blue-grey local stone, as characteristic of older Somerset as are thatch of old Dorset or rag-stone of old Kent. It mellows beautifully, and lasts for centuries. The enclosing walls also are often of stone, topped with a broken pattern of long and short stones not unlike battlements. With age, they begin to harbour attractive rock plants and mosses. A noticeable feature of the area is the tendency to build blocks of cottages sideways-on to the roads instead of facing straight; new houses and flats still sometimes follow this traditional ground plan, even though they are no longer entirely of stone.

A much loved feature of the older type cottage of the Polden and Mendip districts, such as those still extant on Street's outer perimeter, is the deep stone chimney corner. There is nothing pleasanter in winter than to sit close to an open fire of logs and local peat, within these cosy stone corners. I once met a couple who had decided against moving to a lovely labour-saving new home from a centuries-old house near Street, because neither could develop any enthusiasm for functional square walls without the old chimney corner. The inside walls of these cottages are very thick and cool; those of one of my Street homes were adorned only with colourwash slopped on by Mother or myself from a pigswill bucket, and the floors too were of stone, while the plumbing was outside what is known as the back-house; one extra severe winter icicles 9in. long dangled from the outdoor tap yet there was never a burst. Such is the strength of the mature Somerset house, while certain contemporary buildings may develop cracks, sags, or suspect flooring.

The days of chimney corners and stone floors are now over, and little quarrying is done for house building, but most of the modern houses arising in and near Street today have an element of the country style about their low comfortable proportions.

Another central Somerset characteristic is the neat little square central porch, again common to many of the more mature cottages, often having a small pointed roof; plenty still stand on Street's outskirts and around the Polden area. Such porches may sometimes be enclosed to form a diminutive scullery.

I was pleasantly surprised on my latest return visit to discover that, once away from the town centre, attractive smallholdings and pleasant country style residences were as much in evidence as ever, and that the meadows were as lushly green and buttercup filled. Much had altered in the town itself, generally for the better, but in the country life seemed much as it was decades ago; apart from the increasing elaboration of farm machinery and farm management, the land changes slowly.

A few insights into the farming and smallholding sides of its activity help give a balanced picture of Street not merely as a model factory town but a threefold personality: an agricultural community on its outskirts, a lively shopping centre with an exceptional wealth of public amenities, and the home of world-famous industries.

Sedgemoor and Athelney
Battlefields and Burnt Cakes

"HISTORY is bunk", said Henry Ford, a sentiment with which the average scholar would agree if his teachers have fed him on strings of dates. Clothed with the flesh and blood of realism, history is far from being bunk; it is action, excitement, cruelty and kingship, great deeds and bloody ones, defeats and achievements, the famous, the infamous, the saints and the frauds.

Somerset schoolchildren are less likely than most to go forward into adulthood thinking history dull, living as they do near the very scenes of some of the most stirring events in English history. At Athelney an army was raised before marching to victory, and on Sedgemoor a rebel army was defeated; local history also adds the Reformation, the Civil War and the Bloody Assize. Then there were the kings: Alfred the chronicler-king who led that Athelney army to the triumph of Ethandune, Arthur the partly legendary king whom modern discoveries have clothed with a little more substance, and Monmouth the sham pretender-king, who was proclaimed king, defeated at Sedgemoor and executed in rapid succession. What could be less dull than such a calendar?

If we had no history books to say otherwise, we might find it difficult to believe that Sedgemoor's silent acres had ever echoed to clashing weapons and warring shouts; we should notice only its peaceful beauty, and be content with that. Though it covers about 120 square miles, and includes a number of villages, man on the moors is conspicuous by his absence; the lark pours out a song any coloratura soprano might envy, for only the cows to hear. The chink of milk churns and the barking of farm dogs may well be the only other sounds.

If you would find true peace in silence that is serene but not dreary, the inner hearts of the Somerset moors are among the areas in our rushing swirl of humanity where it may yet be found. Not long ago, I heard two countrywomen from this area discussing a third, about to leave for the capital: "Arr, she be really thrilled. She's never been on a train, and she's never been to London". Perhaps it was an isolated case, I decided, but only a month afterwards found myself meeting another lady, also making her first visit to London. It is refreshing to know that such pockets of unsophisticated refuge from modernity exist. The villages of Sedgemoor have grown in recent decades, notably Weston Zoyland as a dormitory town for Bridgwater, attracting not only local buyers but also people whose business lies in the towns but who prefer quietness for their homes; nevertheless, the actual moorlands remain gloriously undisturbed by modernity.

Like much of central Somerset, Sedgemoor once formed the bottom of the lagoon stretching inland beyond Avalon, as its almost complete flatness testifies. A glance at a contoured map reveals roundish or oblong tracts of land spaced across this smooth floor, the islands where stand the villages. At first sight they may appear as islands still among the tidal wash of swaying summer grasses, undulating in long rhythmic waves to the breeze.

We cannot truly ascertain the area's exact form in pre-history, but being fairly near the present coastline we may conjecture that whereas the farthest inland parts of the old sea probably petered out into marshland, this part nearer the open sea may rather have been a broad expanse of clear water with marshy tracts at its edges, perhaps not unlike the island-strewn reaches of present-day Poole Harbour. Winter floods sometimes give some picture of Sedgemoor's old face, though modern drainage methods have considerably reduced their occurrence during the last few years. If the floods do come, villages and farms, on the ancient isles or banks, stand disconsolately isolated while winter winds brush the shallow waters into long-lined ripples. There are no hedges or walls, except of course round property and villages, but wooden gates or fences mark where field entrances cross the rhynes by narrow cattle-bridges. In times of flood they stand apparently without visible use, sticking forlornly from the water.

It is believed that the Saxons made attempts at drainage, and more was certainly done in the Middle Ages. In 1606 came a major inundation when floods backed by exceptional tides swept the sea into its old haunts, drowning farms and flooding the centre of Bristol among other towns. The event has not been forgotten, nor should it be; the sea is a powerful enemy who may suddenly turn on man's defences. Here is a parallel with Holland; like the Dutch, Somerset people realise that the sea "bears watching".

As in Holland, there is a crisscross pattern of intersecting dykes, the rhynes, with a number of bigger defences or drains, of which the King's Sedgemoor Drain is among the most important. The rhynes divide as well as drain the land; looking down from a height one has an impression of a gigantic geometrical diagram marked off by thin silver lines, as if the countryside had been laid out according to set-square and ruler. Along the rhynes grow the inevitable lines of pollarded willows, their delicate foliage drooping languidly, the only things of any height apart from the tall church towers belonging to lowland countries, to East Anglia, Flanders and the Netherlands as well as Somerset.

Another noticeable group of growing things are the reeds, osiers, sedges and withies, certain of them being cultivated for the still extant cottage craft of basket making. Despite contemporary machine-made goods, this hand-made basketry finds a market, and is pursued around Athelney and Burrow Bridge. Bound bundles of the drying sticks are a familiar sight beneath the willows. The industry's heyday came with the Victorian fashion for wickerwork in anything from tables to babies' cots, but survives in a modest way even now.

Teazles too are cultivated, particularly south of Athelney, sharply prickled heads of clinging teeth. This clinging and scratching property makes the teazle useful in cloth-making, for "teasing" or combing tweeds to raise the nap. Machinery cannot yet better the humble teazle at this job, and there is thus some demand for its services.

A minor and perhaps less attractive commercial proposition was once Sedgemoor eels, in which Langport did notable trade.

Cultivation apart, reeds of several kinds grow freely on the moors, standing stiffly upright in clumps, audibly rattling in a moderate wind. Even now I cannot resist the juvenile habit of splitting the tubelike fleshy stems to reveal the spongey white substance inside these interesting plants. Moorland wild flowers have their own special beauty; patches of deep gold gleam from shallow ditches, the big kingcups for which many a youngster had a muddy ducking, so attractive are the gilded cups just out of reach. There are wild yellow irises in thick clumps, and that most beloved of flowers to the exiled sentimentalist, the meadow-sweet; as scented as its name implies, it consists of feathery fronds of tiniest cream blossoms. In the meadows are found long-stemmed cowslips, delicate mauve cuckoo flowers, and a summer carpet of buttercups.

Even a few steps up an incline, probably leading to the higher ground on which stand the villages, some mere hamlets while others are growing and changing, opens a wonderful panorama. One can appreciate the utter regularity of the terrain, and the sharply outlined islands.

Sedgemoor and Athelney have the hauntingly individual beauty belonging to lowlands, where sky and earth meet at infinity. Herds of cattle graze all over the landscape. Here is seen a characteristic Somerset sight, the cow-procession, like a plodding desert caravan on the skyline. When their natural alarm clocks foretell milking time, the heavy beasts turn towards the farm, lumbering in long slow files with bovine leisureliness along the straight tracks running like causeways above the low-lying fields.

Cows are the leading form of livestock, Sedgemoor being a major dairying district. Plodding along a lane, they prove to have only three speeds: slow, dead slow, and stop. As a road block, they are extremely effective, meandering from left to right with the vagueness of creatures with all day to spare. There are only two answers for the motorist who finds himself sharing the road: if he is a townsman, to drum impatient fingers and curse, if he is a countryman to sit back, light a pipe and "let 'em be".

Buildings may show one noticeable difference compared with those of the Polden country; they are often of brick instead of the familiar stone, a reminder that Bridgwater, the capital and gateway to Sedgemoor and the Parrett hinterland, was among other things a brick-making town. Standing where the tidal Parrett could conveniently be crossed, its geographical position made Bridgwater a port and town of consequence in the Middle Ages.

Bridgwater's great natural attraction is the Parrett bore, twice daily. Less well known than the Severn bore, it is worth seeing in its own right; at the spring tides the wave may be up to six feet high.

As befits a port, Bridgwater gave at least one of her sons to naval history, Admiral Blake, born here in 1598. Being an important route-town, as any map reveals at a glance, it once had a defensive castle, destroyed following the Civil War by the Roundheads. The Royalists had held it, despite Bridgwater's Parliamentary leaning.

At Bridgwater the Duke of Monmouth and his followers spent their last night before the disaster of Sedgemoor; Monmouth it is told, climbed the tower of one of its churches to study the lie of the land

Sedgemoor seen from the Polden Hills above Street.

that fatal evening.

The town is famous also for its annual Guy Fawkes carnivals in November, to which thousands flock from miles around. The procession of floats takes hours to pass any given point. Over a thousand people form the procession, watched by almost the entire population as well as the innumerable visitors; shopkeepers prudently board up their windows in advance. A highlight is the traditional squibbing contest, using specially-made giant squibs; the air becomes charged with smoke, the smell of gunpowder, and satisfyingly loud bangs. If the object is to produce as fiery a spectacle as Guy Fawkes himself planned, Bridgwater makes a most valiant effort to achieve it, at huge cost; the expenditure on fireworks must be astronomical.

Before both the Roundheads and Monmouth lived a man who was to make his mark on English history, as far back as the 9th century: King Alfred. To most of us the two memorable stories concerning him are the victory of Ethandune and the burning of the cakes, both of which are associated with the Athelney area. At Athelney Alfred finally rallied the army which was to win the victory that had so far eluded him, a failure which understandably occupied his deepest thoughts. From one such mood of depression comes the immortal episode of the burnt cakes, recounted with suitable localised embroidery. Basically the tale goes that Alfred, wandering pensively in the lonely marshes near Athelney, came upon a cottage. Suddenly aware that exercise and thought had raised an appetite, he asked the old lady within for a snack, omitting to add that he was the king. Luckily she was actually baking some cakes, which she suggested the visitor might watch until they were ready, while she went out. Alfred sat by the hearth, and his thoughts returned again to the Danes; there must be a solution to the problem. Deeper he pondered, the cakes unheeded. The old lady, returning to a smell of burning, roundly scolded this man-like lapse with the thoroughness of a countrywoman to whom a batch of spoilt cakes were no small loss. It is interesting to speculate how she took the discovery that he was the king. The cottage's site is uncertain, but this did not deter at least one teller of tall tales, unversed in both historical and architectural periods, from lately pointing out to me a blatantly 18th century cottage as the scene of the cakes' incineration.

In assessing the magnitude of King Alfred's achievement, we should realise that the Danes had already overrun East Anglia, Northumberland and Mercia, holding a large slice of southern England in their grasp. Wessex was the next victim. The invader, after resisting several attempts by Alfred to dislodge him, must have felt in a strong position, perhaps underestimating Alfred's singleminded determination to overcome him yet. Again the king assembled his forces, this time among Athelney's marshes, in the year 878, to march for Ethandune and another encounter. It was an ideal rallying place, centred on two good strongholds, Athelney itself and the smaller Burrow Mump.

A strange hillock is The Mump, crowned by a ruined medieval church. To see it at dusk is to feel pleasantly eerie shudders, provoked by the spooky outline of the old ruin above the hill's soft blue-black outline. If ever a hill was made to be haunted, it was surely this ancient look-out, from which King Alfred almost certainly surveyed his surroundings when finalising his planned march to Ethandune and victory. The exact site of that important encounter seems to be unknown, but is generally understood to have been two days' march east from Athelney, bearing out the supposition that it was over the border in Wiltshire.

As we know, Ethandune was the decisive struggle, and the end of the Danes' plan to annexe most of England. Their leader accepted defeat with reluctant grace, in what is known as the Treaty of Wedmore, Wedmore being another of the central Somerset ridges, a long finger of land similarly formed to the Polden Hills. Alfred was no tyrant in victory; rather, he sought to overlay bad with good, insisting that Guthrum the Dane should be baptised.

King Alfred, true to the tradition of olden times, built an abbey in thanksgiving for victory. Some say that, overshadowed by Glastonbury and others, it died and left no trace above ground, others that the present church of Lyng may incorporate fragments. One marvellous relic of King Alfred has been found and identified, the beautifully wrought ornament called Alfred's Jewel, now safely preserved in the Ashmolean Museum at Oxford. This delicately chased piece, one of the best finds recorded in the area, is fashioned of gold and enamel, and inscribed: "Alfred had me to be made".

Warlike activity disturbed the peace again with the Civil War, fought with considerable bitterness in Somerset, but it was the Battle of Sedgemoor that became one of the best known episodes not only in local but in national history. The finest general views of the famous battlefield are from the Polden Hills, including the superb panoramas from above Street and Walton, stretching also to the far Quantocks. Farther along the Polden ridge we can stand above the actual site of the battle. Since then the King's Sedgemoor Drain has altered the ground plan considerably, while the strategically vital Bussex Rhyne has, on the other hand, disappeared; all the same, visiting the scene adds reality to the story. Ideally one should come by moonlight, as this is said to have been the battle's actual lighting.

Sedgemoor, the last battle fought on English soil, was the culmination of a futile bid for the Throne by the illegitimate son of Charles II, the Duke of Monmouth. Monmouth had earlier been accepted at Court, following the usual social round and living in a style suggesting that he already thought and lived in regal manner. Pepys, writing in 1663, describes the marriage of "the little Duke of Monmouth" which took place "at White Hall in the King's chamber". That evening the new bridegroom threw a grand ball and supper at his home near, Charing Cross; Pepys reporting it notes that his coach bore "the arms of England, Scotland, and France, quartered upon some other fields", but adds "what it is that speaks of his being a bastard I know not". Three years later Pepys did know; writing of the King's amours he remarks; "the King hath many bastard children that are known and owned, besides the Duke of Monmouth". Charles, leaving no legitimate heir, had been succeeded by his brother James II, who quickly antagonised both people and Parliament with his stubbornness and Catholic views. At the time of his accession Monmouth was exiled in Europe, but was already regarded by some

45

English Protestants as a likely leader against James and his religion. In June 1685 he returned, landing at Lyme Regis, a Puritan stronghold.

Marching across Somerset, Monmouth gathered a sizeable force to his side, mainly yeomen and small traders; the higher born, knowing him to be a bastard, could not seriously accept him as a pretender to the Throne of England. Purporting to have evidence that he was in fact of legitimate birth, Monmouth was proclaimed king in the West Country.

The entire rebellion was essentially a Somerset affair fought by Somerset men on their home ground, carried on the tide of Monmouth's ambition and his supposed championship of their Puritanism. Poorly armed and schooled neither in combat nor military discipline, their best weapons were their devotion and their yeoman courage. It was a futile cause from the start; how could one man of doubtful birth, backed by a few thousand countrymen, storm London to win the Crown? Soon the King's troops were on their trail; when they reached Bridgwater, the army was only a few miles off, camped at Weston Zoyland, on Sedgemoor. Here the two sides were to meet on July 6th, 1685.

Even at the eleventh hour Monmouth had a scheme: to surprise the troops in camp by night, from a completely unlikely angle. Accordingly at midnight "King" Monmouth and his men slipped out of Bridgwater by moonlight. The lane down which they marched that fateful night bears the appropriate title of War Lane. Once on the moors they had one invaluable asset, their knowledge of the country, the layout of ditches, fields and causeways. Silently they crept on, until the great Bussex Rhyne barred their path. Searching for a crossing place, they were suddenly plunged into war; one of their own men's weapons had gone off accidentally in the silent night, rousing the army encamped only yards away beyond the Rhyne. Their first salvoes sent Monmouth's untrained horses in flight, fleeing with the precious ammunition carts. The outcome was inevitable, courage not being enough in the face of military arms and training.

The Battle of Sedgemoor raged between about 1 and 2 a.m. and, to borrow a phrase beloved of boxing commentators: "It was all over" in an hour and a half. During those 90 minutes, 16 of the King's men died, and no less than 300 rebels.

So ended one slaughter, to be followed by another. Many of the defeated were straightaway shot or hanged, adding their numbers to the dead already littering the fatal field. Graveyard Field is a local name for one of these burial places of the slain.

Next day another 500 were herded to Weston Zoyland church, to languish until the following dawn; many were wounded, some died there; about a score were, it is told, hung in chains from the church battlements, a detail lovingly recounted to interested visitors who stop to view the site of the bloodbath.

While the half-thousand wounded prisoners groaned within the church that dreadful night, others were made to construct the ghastly gibbets or to drag chains intended for the mass hangings to come. Chedzoy church, too, bears reminders of the men who died in this doomed venture; its walls are marked where Monmouth's men reputedly sharpened their weapons against the stones.

Survivors in scores were hanged following the battle. The Somerset lanes that eventful day became a vast butchery where sides of human flesh hung from trees or gibbets. Monmouth himself was not there to witness the spectacle, having fled to the New Forest where he was found cowering in a ditch. The tree overhanging the spot became known as Monmouth's Ash. His intention had been to lie low in the Forest before quietly sailing out of Lymington into exile, but it was not to be. The Tower of London lay ahead of him instead of a royal palace, and his head was destined for the chopping block instead of the Crown.

The thick cover of the New Forest beckoned fugitives from the broken army as Monmouth himself. Some found shelter there with sympathisers who, if the truth was discovered, paid dearly for their charity, such as the kindly Dame Alice Lyle who perished for harbouring some escaping rebels, at the order of the ruthless Judge Jeffreys.

The living were rewarded with some of the most brutal punishment ever meted out in England, by "that devil incarnate" Judge Jeffreys. A spate of executions followed hurried trials, while others were sold into slavery, given impossible fines, or sentenced to savage floggings. The Bloody Assize did not acquire that name for nothing. It is a small consolation to recall that the "devil incarnate" himself met his end in the Tower only three years after his murderous if legal descent on Somerset in the Bloody Assize, when the tables turned against him, as was the habit of events in that age.

Many villages have tales to tell of the Rebellion. An early connection of the Street Clarks offered hospitality to the Duke himself, who left behind a chest of important papers and the gift of his jewelled snuff box. The farmer, his allegiance becoming known, was among those sentenced by Jeffreys to be hanged. Locking, at the seaward end of the Mendips, remembers that its Lord of the Manor joined the Rebellion with his two sons. Both lads died but the father escaped, returning to Locking to lie low with his favourite dog. The dog's barking betrayed him, and the tale ends with his being hanged in the village. His lady in frenzied grief flung the dog down a deep well in the manor grounds, and herself after it. The moor itself is naturally said to harbour the spirits of the dead, though few essay to prove the point after dark. The battle took place by night, so the probability is that, if ghosts exist at all, they must walk this tragic scene after the descent of dusk.

Retribution against Monmouth's supporters was by no means limited to the Sedgemoor and Polden areas, or even to Somerset; as far away as southern Dorset, three Swanage men who had fought for him were hung, drawn and quartered by the King's soldiers, at a quarry locally known by the gruesome if appropriate name, Gallows Gore. Nearby Wareham has a Bloody Bank, the scene of a typical post-Sedgemoor, post-Jeffreys multiple execution, though it lies on the far side of another county.

So died the tumult of the Monmouth Rebellion. The fight was lost. Sedgemoor knew no more of war, minor disturbances apart, until the 20th century. Then, the village to which so many were dragged in defeat took its place in another war, a wider and more national conflict; the war in the air. RAF Weston Zoyland played its part in intercepting aircraft bound for the prime targets of Bristol and the industry of South Wales.

County of contrast, the introduction to this volume called Somerset, a term very applicable to the countryside of Sedgemoor and Athelney. Geographically there is the same difference as between Avalon and its surroundings, where the Polden islands stand above the uniform grasslands. The country has on its surface the complete peace of wide open space, where one cow mooing carries on the clear air, yet one of the bloodiest battles ever waged on English soil was fought here by amateurs against professional troops, hopelessly outclassed but to be admired for their loyalty to their leader's impossible campaign.

The sandwich of war and peace, war again and peace again, seems to be woven into the enigmatic quality of Sedgemoor.

The Polden Country
Red Apples and Rough Justice

EXTREMES of human belief and behaviour match Somerset's topographical variety. Sedgemoor, though now among the quietest stretches of unspoiled countryside, echoed to one of the goriest British battles, followed by vicious retribution; the Polden Hills, looking down upon the historic field of carnage, likewise have a background of intermingled violence and peace, witnessing the emergence of Quakerism as well as the aftermath of Sedgemoor and the fighting between neighbour and neighbour during the Civil War.

Polden personalities are no less diverse, ranging from the founder of Pennsylvania to a notable British naval dynasty, a sad young bride whose fate lives in an immortal traditional ballad, and a leading figure in the development of the English novel.

Doubtless one reason for the Polden Hills' continuing pastoral nature is the lack of major tourist attractions, apart from the fine views across the fields marking the site of the Battle of Sedgemoor; there is no cathedral or ruined abbey, no stately homes, no Cheddar or Wookey Hole; to country lovers such a lack is itself the Poldens' beauty, because where there are no coach parties there are no snackbars, tramping feet or roaring wheels. It is a restful district, and a revelation to the visitor who, having come to Somerset, finds himself in company with the hot-dog munching crowds of the coastal resorts and the trippers' paradises, until he realises that there is another Somerset not very far inland, the Somerset of grey stone walls and farming country.

The hills appear insignificant at first; not so, such hills form a long low ridge jutting out onto the moors where the sea once washed the island shores. Ancient man lived either at the fringes of those dry sanctuaries in a damp marshy world, or on the higher land where he

Westcountry History: Somerset

could grow food, rear cattle, and see enemies approaching. The Romans, too, used any tracts of drier land to build roads – such as that running parallel with the causeway between Street and Glastonbury – paving some of them with stone from the Polden Hills. Human habitation is still mainly confined to definitely defined village communities, situated towards the bottom of the slopes rather than on the actual hilltops, the majority on the northern or gentle dip-slope side; there are noticeably fewer settlements on the southern scarp-face of the hills.

Change and development are an inevitable part of modern life: yesterday's beauty spot is too often today's housing estate. Revisiting a loved spot after twenty years to find it unchanged is all too rare a pleasure, making such refuges as the heights of the Poldens the more precious. New housing appears in old villages, as is only to be expected, but the hills themselves come as near as possible to standing still. This I discovered one spring when returning to a part of the Poldens I had not seen since teenagehood; unbelievably the same stile, its rickety woodwork apparently still unmended as I remembered it last, led to the same slopes where grow lady's slipper, wild thyme, and myriad tiny plants peeping shyly from tall fluttering grasses. The peace was blessedly unchanged, broken only by the distant voices of farm dogs and the cuckoo's maddening monotonous call from the woods. Suddenly there was a swish and a rustle as a lovely red-brown rabbit shot from the undergrowth, stared for a moment, and scampered off like the rabbit of Alice in Wonderland remembering: "I'm late". Yes, the fauna also was the same, right down to the scattered evidence of rabbit occupation descriptively known as bunny-bullets.

Even the bus ride up to the old haunt had been a pleasure after city crowds and city tempers, starting with four passengers, three of whom departed en route. According to the timetable a convenient return bus was due in just over an hour. "Aw arr, that's me", the driver confirmed; apparently there was but one bus trundling back and forth a few times a day. "Don't 'ee worry, Miss. I'll be looking out for 'ee" the friendly charioteer insisted, anxious to save his solitary passenger a long tramp. It all seemed impossibly far removed from teeming crowds going tensely about a life they must pretend is important no matter how humdrum the routine of their little claustrophobic offices may be.

Polden life is country life, the world of the farm and orchard. Dairying is important on these well-drained slopes that have at the same time sufficient moisture to produce rich grazing pastureland. During the late summer the cider-apple trees are covered with small scarlet fruit, growing in clusters that glow as if their skins were painted and polished a clear bright red. The cider-apples in central Somerset are as typical of their area as hops are in Kent, bringing a note of gaiety to their green surroundings at harvest time. The hills support most forms of arable farming, such as wheat and barley, fruit and market gardening. The cornfields lie on the gentle dip-slope side, but the alert-eyed walker can spot a lot more than corn there when tramping the footpaths running through the straight stalks; there are the scarlet pimpernels or poor man's weatherglasses, tightly shut if rain threatens, but a tiny spot of scarlet when opened to greet fine weather; poppies in the corn are a delight to the walker, though less popular with the farmer whose crop they invade; perhaps loveliest of all are the wild pansies, miniature replicas of the garden variety but only about a half inch across, like little elves' faces grinning between the corn stalks.

Other wild flowers are many and various, especially the smaller gems that do not assault the casual eye as does the buttercup, but lie under foot to be sought out: the pale yellow rockrose, the bugloss, the blue speedwell and the cheeky little eyebright. The early purple orchid is reasonably common, but the rarer bee-orchid is a more exciting find.

Wild flowers, growing crops, and dairy cattle: these are the stuff of the Poldens' charm; the very sight of placidly grazing cows is as good as the best sedative.

One of the loveliest forms of young life is the newly hatched chick, a ball of yellow fluff the shape of an egg, cheeping for food. I never forgot the farmer who held an egg in his hand while I watched a crack appear in the shell, through which poked an enquiring beak; a few moments later a bedraggled chick lay triumphantly in the broken shell. Such miracles are among the saddest denials to those who miss a country upbringing; staring at the television in the corner is no substitute for such eternal memories as seeing new life emerge from a common egg.

Another joy is the first lambs of springtime; there is sometimes something approaching reverence in the way a rough labourer holds a newborn lamb in his arms, conscious of the marvel of nature even though he has lived with it all his life. Each sheep is a character, farmers assert, some timid, some strong, some bad tempered, some adventurous; one is born to leadership, standing alert at the head of a flock, and may even stamp a petulant foot at the trespasser. Sheep are kept for profit and not as pets, yet some owners develop a real affection for them; a prosperous farmer, leaning on the field gate surveying his flock one evening, once told me they were to be sold next day. He would not be there: he planned a trip to Taunton, theoretically for shopping but really, he confessed, because he hated seeing them go. He always went out the day a flock was sold, he said. Life on the land and with livestock is one of the enduring things in our rapidly progressing world; mechanisation has replaced the drudgery of scythes and pitchforks, and equipment boasting ever-increasing elaboration is now available as well as a bewildering variety of chemical aids to good cropping, but the broad basis of farming is in itself rooted in the pattern of tradition.

Stone quarrying was until the 20th century an important occupation, stone being the chief building material. The heart of most villages is of weathered stone, only the more modern houses on their outskirts being in more contemporary materials. In the 19th century quarrying came third in importance after shoe-making (in and around Street) and agriculture. Fruit orchards can be seen lying in curiously shaped hollows sunk below the surrounding terrain; they are planted in worked-out quarries which, having the top soil replaced, give ideal shelter for ripening the fruit. The distinctive blue lias in parts of the region, formerly much used for doorsteps and paving stones, is a fossil bearing rock from the age of extraordinary monsters that were half beast and half reptile, armed with awful teeth and giant scaled and spined tails. Fossil specimens unearthed include ichthyosaurus and plesiosaurus, some of which have found their way to museums as far afield as London. Though little stone is now used for building, it has its uses, not least for what is tactfully called monumental masonry; one local mason was so proud of his work as to invite me to look closer at his stock of gravestones before going into the back shed where coffins were being made. If he hoped to test the power of that trump card of commerce, the impulse sale, he was unlucky, my not being in the mood to purchase a tombstone or coffin at the time.

If you would hear Zummerzet As She Is Spoke, one of the best places to hear the genuine dialect is the Polden country, far removed from the commercialised parts of Somerset. West Country speech, exaggerated by comedians as an alternative to Cockney or over-broad Lancashire, is in its native environment a normal means of communication, the language of the shop, bus-queue and kerbside. One can hardly blame impersonators adopting this picturesque vocabulary, as there is undeniable fascination about Devon and Somerset phraseology. "How be y'on?" means "How are you?", to which the answer may be "Fair to middling", meaning anything from on top of the world to the depths of Monday miseries. Another common remark is "That shook 'ee"; a neighbour's small boy who delighted to spring at people from behind trees shouting "That shook 'ee" thus invented a new name for Mother, Ma Tookee. "Aw arr" is not, as certain entertainers suggest, a muck-spreader's expression, but simply a Somerset affirmative. "Without a word of a lie I be telling 'ee the truth" is the prelude to a village liar's next tall story. "Ee can't get the better of Oi" reveals the canny businessman under the son-of-the-soil exterior, much the same as "Oi bain't going to be put upon" or "Oi bain't skeerd of 'ee".

Asking the way of a countryman may produce an interesting assortment of Somerset expressions if not the required information. He will probably say, "Arr, 'ee be just up and round", and up and round may be up the street and around the next corner, a mile to the north, or an hour's tramp towards nowhere. Always beware of being told a place is "up and round" or: "'Ee be only a couple o' miles": that means country miles, probably four by the map.

Most people who know the West Country even casually are aware that this attractive and individual manner of speech exists, but fewer appear to observe an equally striking feature of the people themselves: Somerset hair. It is a localised western beauty which city sophisticates would give a year's hairdressing bills to acquire, not red, but a clear, clean shining gold, sometimes described as corn-coloured, and having lovely thickness and sheen. Men also may be so blessed; lately I met a large man whose thick corn-coloured waves any woman could have snatched from his head with envy, even if she did not covet the matching beard.

From the casual visitor's angle, the main interest of the Polden Hills is most likely to be the succession of breathtaking views embracing most of Somerset. Ivythorn Hill above Street, in the National Trust's care, is among the finest, noted also for the lovely woods that are well stocked with primroses and bluebells, and the white violet as well as the mauve variety. There are splendid visions across Sedgemoor to the distant Quantocks, and as far as Dorset: in clear weather I have had Portland Bill pointed out. Nature is so generous that she gives Ivythorn Hill double measure, adding equally fine prospects in the other direction towards the Mendips, Glastonbury Tor dominating a vastness of green country. The entire sweep of the central moorlands spreads towards the sea, as flat as a green carpet. In the far distance another solitary island mass, Brent Knoll, breaks the skyline where the silver streak of the Bristol Channel shows in late afternoon when the sun, moving over the sea, turns it to a glittering mirror. Clouds chase each other across the country, sometimes drifting lazily as a silently moving patch of darker green, sometimes scurrying as if the shadows were taking part in a cross-country run; thus one can watch the movements of the clouds underfoot as well as overhead. It is an intensely English scene, summing up all that is meant by "England's green and pleasant land". But walk a little farther along the ridge towards the Somerton cross-roads, and this green and pleasant land, paradoxical, unpredictable Somerset, springs one of its contradictory surprises; standing on a very English hilltop is a Swiss chalet. The core is basically an ordinary country house, but it is faced with dark timbered balconies and deep chalet eaves. On the first floor long windows fold open onto the wide wooden balcony, and the floor above is half hidden under the eaves. The roof was so designed to collect rain-water, there being no piped water available on the hill; whether there is any real connection with Switzerland I have been unable to discover. The chalet was built by two Quaker sisters and presented by them to the Society of Friends for public rest, recuperation, refreshment and social life. Architects would doubtless call the chalet a freak or folly, but it is an attractive one to find on so un-Swiss a hill. By a strange coincidence I was reminded of it one day in the real Swiss Alps, when gazing at a stupendous panorama of mountains and gorges, almost level with the line of the eternal snow. As often happens other walkers fell into conversation, as people will in so majestic a place, talking in any languages they could collectively muster; they included a German hiker whose anorak was decorated with tourist badges from most of Europe; between Paris and Naples he wore a badge embroidered with a Swiss chalet and inscribed "Street, Somerset". Meeting this Polden curiosity on a genuine Swiss pass was the kind of coincidence that is too extraordinary to be anything but true.

Prominent atop the Polden Hills from many miles around is the slim column above Butleigh, erected to one of the distinguished naval family of Hoods, Admiral Sir Samuel Hood. The column, usually referred to simply as Butleigh Monument or the Hood Monument, is topped by a naval crown, and the woods on one side are so placed as to perfectly frame a cameo of Glastonbury Tor. The naval saga of Butleigh began in 1741 when, in the romantic dare-devil manner of the age, the two young sons of the local vicar went off to sea. Both rose to the top of the Service, becoming Viscount Hood and Lord Bridport. The memorial at Butleigh is to yet another seafaring Hood, whose epitaph in Butleigh church was composed by no less a poet than Southey; the column records that he was "an officer of the highest distinction among the illustrious men who rendered their own age the brightest period in the naval history of their country". Hood believed in asking of his subordinates no more than he would do himself; seeing the sailors hesitate to put out into a stormy ocean to rescue three shipwreck victims, he jumped into the boat with them, showing that he would never give an order he was not himself prepared to carry out. Nelson called him "the best officer ... England has to boast of"; what man of the sea could receive a finer tribute than these words from the "great little Admiral" in person?

The hill where the Hood Monument stands is barely 300 feet above sea level, but the lowness of the surrounding country gives it an artificial impressiveness. I have sat here watching cricket played what seemed a long way below, seeing the ball leave the bat a noticeable interval before the sound of ball against bat reached the car, a phenomenon caused by the clearness of the air, and the relative height above the widespread open country.

In the grounds of Butleigh Court is a healthy offshoot from the Holy Thorn of Glastonbury, flowering like its parent tree in the winter as well as in May.

Bawdrip may not be a familiar name, even to West Country folk, but a story connected with the village is told in a ballad sung at Christmas throughout England, "The Mistletoe Bough". The heroine, "young Lovell's bride", a daughter of the rector, was married in the local church a few hours before the famous disappearance at her wedding feast. The tale is too familiar to need more than brief repetition: suffice it to repeat that the young bride conceived the gay prank of hiding herself in an old chest to mystify her husband and guests, laughingly calling: "And Lovell be sure thou'rt the first to trace the clue to my secret lurking place". She slipped inside the heavy chest, and the lock clicked fast; too late she found it impossible to open from the inside. The girl's amusing play had left her in what was to be her tomb, her desperate cries unheard while the guests searched high and low. We can only guess what agony of mind the youthful bride suffered, entombed alive within reach of help, her shouts deadened by the hefty old lid. Not until many years afterwards was the mystery solved, when the chest was opened by a new generation of the family: as the gruesome ballad records: "They raised the lid, And a skeleton form lay mouldering there, In the bridal wreath of the lady fair". All those long years "Her bridal bloom Lay withering there in a living tomb". The sad story of the bride of Bawdrip has gone forever into English song in this rather macabre song, "The Mistletoe Bough".

Chilton Polden has no such unhappy stories to tell, but is worth seeking out for the fine views from Cock Hill – like Ivythorn Hill, in the care of the National Trust – an endless expanse of green to the far Blackdown and Quantock Hills, rivalling landscapes seen from far greater heights thanks to its placing in relationship to the surrounding hills and plains.

Moorlynch (sometimes spelled Moorlinch) has notable viewpoints, too, including prospects over the battlefield of Sedgemoor. From here the local populace watched dawn break on that tragic scene following a harrowing night of one-sided fighting between Monmouth's enthusiastic but undisciplined followers and drilled professional troops. Near Moorlynch is one of the few woods of any size in this district of uninterrupted openness, Loxley Woods, traversed by a Roman Road. Swayne's Leaps, a series of stones in Loxley Woods, are so named from a hunted Sedgemoor survivor. Swayne, caught by soldiers with a sporting streak, was offered his freedom if he could make three stupendous jumps; terror gave him wings to fly to liberty. Alternatively, Swayne made the leaps that his family, also captured, should remember his last athletic moments; the duped guards, agreeing, saw Swayne disappear into the woods to freedom. I was once told the story in Loxley Woods at silent eerie twilight; so should all such tales be heard, in a macabre forest at dusk.

Edington, another Polden village, claims to be the site of the Battle of Ethandune when King Alfred's soldiers vanquished the Danish invader. Another Edington, that in Wiltshire, also considers itself the scene of that important encounter; as Ethandune was about two days' march east from Athelney, where Alfred's army had assembled, the Wiltshire claim is the more likely; Edington, Somerset, could have been reached from Athelney by a marching army within hours rather than days.

The wealthy Abbots of Glastonbury had several local country homes showing remarkably secular splendour, such as the beautiful Ivythorn Manor, situated at the feet of the Polden Hills facing directly across the airy open spaces of Sedgemoor. Another such house was erected at Sharpham by Abbot Bere, a house of double destiny. It was from here that the frail and aged last Abbot, Richard Whiting, was dragged as a prisoner accused by the Commissioners of withholding the Glastonbury treasures, to be shuttled from the Tower of London to a mockery of a trial at Wells, and finally to a traitor's death on the Tor, following which his white-haired head was exhibited atop his own abbey gateway. The martyred Abbot is recalled on Glastonbury's present town map, in a Whiting Road.

The same house at Sharpham saw the birth of Henry Fielding in 1707, the author of "Tom Jones" among other evergreen works. Fielding is considered by literary authorities to be one of the founders, following Defoe, of the English novel as we understand it now, paving the way to the golden age of English writing in the later 18th and early 19th centuries. He was one of the first to combine storytelling with rounded studies of character and emotion, peopling his books with flesh-and-blood human beings instead of creatures of unlikely romance, unattainable virtue, or impossible badness. Fielding's novels "Tom Jones", "Joseph Andrews" and "Amelia" are compulsory standard landmarks for modern students of literature or librarianship.

The first also remains thoroughly gripping reading for the more average person; as a beautifully photographed film this story conceived over two centuries earlier enjoyed considerable popular success in the 1960s, and again as a television drama in the 1990s. From Fielding's pen also came everyday phrases still in use, such as "sober as a judge" and "roast beef of England". It is interesting to note that at least two immortals of the novel have Somerset connections: Thackeray also worked in the county, writing parts of his best-known books at Clevedon on the Bristol Channel coast.

The development of Quakerism is a most important factor in the story of the Polden area, whose 17th century yeoman farmers were among the first openly to adopt that faith despite considerable opposition to the growth of the sect. It was not unknown for a man to suffer personal violence or even imprisonment for attending a meeting of the Friends. Nevertheless the cult grew and prospered, and the district remains a Quaker stronghold. An early connection of the Street Clarks married a daughter of the greatest Quaker, William Penn. Penn, born in 1644, was founder of Pennsylvania across the Atlantic. Begun in 1682 by Penn as a Quaker colony and refuge, it became the second State of the U.S.A. Many who followed Penn were Polden families, and distant connections live there still. My own family on the paternal grandparents' side is of Polden extraction, and connected by descent with Penn, the name Penn still running in the family. Much though he is respected now in retrospect, Penn's early Somerset days were far from smooth; he was once arrested for preaching to a vast assembly outside the Crown at Wells.

The actual founder of the Society of Friends, or Quakers, was George Fox, whose creed was that men could aspire towards perfection through an inward and personal experience; his journal is the classic expounding of that belief. Fox, like many founder members, suffered persecution and saw his fair share of prison life in the various penal institutions periodically offering him enforced board and lodging. The word Quakerism is said to have been spontaneously invented by one of the judges before whom Fox appeared, to whom the accused had given the somewhat startling advice that he should himself "quake at the name of the Lord".

Hounding these genuine believers of a novel new faith was not the only smear on the face of the Polden country; violence and bloodshed have more than once been seen on these quiet slopes. The first fatal encounter of the Civil War took place at Marshall's Elm, when six hundred men drawn up near this spot on foot met with a body of horsemen from the opposing side. The ensuing encounter was a complete and humiliating fiasco for the Parliamentary forces who marched straight into a clever ambush in a hollow near this place, routed by the charging horsemen. The incident ended with a number of dead and dying, and a fine collection of prisoners and abandoned horses.

This land of little red apples and placid cows saw terrible scenes following the disastrous collapse of the Monmouth Rebellion on Sedgemoor. Next day tired and disillusioned survivors were ruthlessly hunted down, to be shot or hanged on the spot. Many had trudged up onto the hills from the fields of the slain, there to be captured and strung up on any convenient tree; many a lane had a line of gibbets, and many a cross-roads its grisly victims. One mass hanging defiled the fair English scene at Marshall's Elm, the well-known case of the thirty rebels executed together, as bloody a piece of butchery as any recorded of that day. An old record of the period shows how low was the value of human life then: five shillings was the price for "hanging up ye quarters of ye dead men". One hill overlooking the moor is often spoken of as Lollover Hill, a name I have never yet seen on an official map. Local hearsay attributes the name to the despairing cry of defeat: "All over, all over".

Few places outwardly so peaceable have seen more unhappy times than the Polden Hills, in the Civil War, the Monmouth Rebellion and the persecution of the first Quakers, made all the sadder because these were not international political conflicts but wars of neighbour against neighbour, spurred on by the enemies within, hatred and intolerance. More than two centuries after the Battle of Sedgemoor ended in misery and defeat, the Polden Hills saw the end of another war, but one ending in rejoicing instead of carnage. Rejoicing in this case was flashed across Somerset by the time-honoured chain of beacon fires, reviving the practice of centuries ago though the year was 1945, and the message was that of the ending of the Second World War.

Country dwellers often appear to put much more originality and imagination into community events, and Victory Night 1945 was no exception, when the news of peace was sent from the Mendips to the Poldens, from the Poldens to the Quantocks, in a chain of old-style beacons on the hills. Dancing in the streets was but the prelude to a night of revelry, particularly at Street, this being a big enough place to muster crowds to make the evening go with a swing. Everyone with two usable feet was either inside the Crispin Hall doing the Hokey Cokey, or outside in the streets doing an endlessly winding Conga. After dusk most of the population moved off towards the hills, joined by the people of outlying farms and Polden villages. On Ivythorn Hill a lorry-load of free cider waited beside a huge pyramid of sticks, logs, old furniture, disused gates, and anything else burnable. Suddenly from a lonely Mendip height a single light flared, died, then burst into a pinpoint glow; the message was repeated by another, another, and yet another. A whole chain of bonfires began to answer each other across the huge Somerset spaces. A flaming brand was thrust into Ivythorn Hill's waiting pyre, and a long crackling flame flared into the sky taking up the happy news: victory! victory! victory! Dancing round the bonfire was interspersed with enthusiastic swigs at the cider, until the flames were reduced to a circle of cinders and the barrels were empty. Long after midnight the crowd straggled back into Street or to outlying cottages and farms; a few were left by the wayside, smiling blissfully in a cider-tinted stupor, to face a mammoth celebration hangover next morning. Another chapter of history was closed.

Somerset has scenes of far more spectacular appeal than the unassuming Polden Hills, and towns having greater historic interest than the Polden villages, but few parts of this very diverse county have a more generous measure of widespreading views, or offer a pleasanter haven from the sightseeing hordes gathered by the popular places to themselves. The lack of major tourist interest is in itself an asset, preserving the hills' tranquillity. This is not to say that time stands completely still; the smallest local village bows to the square-screened god in the corner of the room, and many villages have their share of new properties surrounding their grey stone cores, but these are steps in time with the world rather than leaps ahead of it for progress' own sake. There remains a whole chain of green hilltops hiding in their long grasses tiny flowers as beautiful in their own way as the extravagant blooms of Chelsea Flower Show, loveliness in miniature like the Poldens themselves.

Polden country is as English as an Elgar march or a Turner landscape; and what could be better reason for exploring some of its small-scale but most appealing charms?

The Central Lowlands
Marsh-men and Milk-churns

HOW did our distant ancestors live, before the civilising influences of Rome and Christianity? Where did they live, what were their homes like, and how did they travel? Archaeology turns up many and varied answers to such questions, but perhaps no part of Britain shows evidence of two such completely opposed ways of ancient life than does central Somerset. True to its nature of contradiction and diversity, it shows early men living in two utter extremes of environment: deep in dark caverns hidden under the Mendips, only seeing the sky when they went forth to hunt; or under the openest of all open skies, that of the central lowlands, in straw and mud huts on artificial platforms in the lakes. The story of the finding of this extraordinary human settlement among the wastes and waters is only one of the many interesting things to be seen and learned about what appears at a passing glance to be a flat, uninteresting plain between one famous landmark and the next.

The lowlands are a region of complete stillness on calm days, but when, as is more usual, the wind sweeps over the limitless nothingness of eternal space, everything is on the move; the rhynes' waters ripple, reeds quiver stiffly with a faint rattle, willow fronds droop, and the endless grass ebbs and flows in long lines like the waves of a pale green lake. There is colour as well as movement; acres of gleaming buttercups, sombre olive-green patches where passing clouds darken the grass they float over, black, white and brown dots that are cows grazing the fertile meadows, and the all-dominant sky of pale shimmering blue rather than the brazen Oxford blue beloved of holidaymakers. There is the beauty of symmetry, too: undeviating straight rhynes, willows like squads of soldiers lined up in exacting formation, their queer truncated forms crowned with the characteristic heads of pollarded willow; reeds standing as stiffly as clutches of knitting needles stuck into the soft earth. Wild yellow irises flower at the rhynes' edges, with creamy meadowsweet and gold kingcups. There is as much beauty on the moors as in the famous beauty-spots, but it is a quieter loveliness that must be sought by the observant eye without the reliance of a guide-book or the commentary of a courier.

The omnipresent Glastonbury Tor dominates all the eastern and central parts of the moors, until the equally noticeable Brent Knoll takes over the work of breaking the horizon nearer the sea. The best way to get a general picture of the moors' immensity and flatness is to climb Glastonbury Tor and study the wondrous panorama towards Brent Knoll and the Bristol Channel; in late afternoon, you may see the Channel itself, shining across the far horizon. From here it is appreciated how few are the villages actually on the moors, and how wide is the green, silver-squared expanse that was the floor of the ancient Somerset lake or sea; a little imagination changing the fields to water and the scattered hills to islands is a useful aid in understanding the former geography of Somerset.

The moors are a refreshing refuge from the city rat-race; nothing can alter the march of progress even here, but it is a march instead of London's headlong stampede. Progress means mechanisation in the milking shed, a car instead of the old pony and trap – though some do still exist in regular use – but not rejection of the old simply because it is old. The moors may be drained and tilled by increasingly mechanical means, but life and speech carry something of yesterday into today.

Wild vegetation and masses of gorse and heather is what most people think of when the word "moor" is mentioned, visualising Scottish highlands or Devon uplands. Nothing could be more unlike wild Scotland or hilly Devon than these Somerset fastnesses calling themselves moors; they resemble much more closely the Dutch polderlands, as anyone familiar with both Holland and Somerset readily notices. The only limit to the open plain is the horizon, in this uniformly level country that is controlled by a system of drainage ditches, perfected over the centuries until the last meres became yet more rich pastureland in the 18th century. It is wonderful grazing country, famous for its dairying, where the cows appear to be legless, much of their figures being hidden in the long grass; milk-churns hold the wealth of the people. On the fringes of the moors where the first contours of the hills or islands appear, the universal cider-apple trees are a froth of blossom in spring and polka-dotted with scarlet in autumn.

An ornithologist's paradise are the moors, where herons flap lazily on heavy wings, and the attractive wagtail zigzags jerkily over the fields, his flight as erratic as a fever-patient's temperature chart except when he periodically stands still, tail wagging up and down true to his name.

Water is ever present; though winter flooding becomes steadily less severe, farmers still wisely site sheds and haystacks on any slight eminence. The builders of the old Somerset and Dorset Railway, realising that most of the land between Glastonbury and Burnham was liable to inundation, raised much of their track a few feet on embankments; old photographs show the little steam trains puffing across these embankments, the Tor in the background, while all around is like the waves of the sea; they might be pictures of Avalon centuries ago, but for the trains.

Drainage is a vital business on these near-sea-level fens, which the sea could well reclaim, given a chance, as the great flood of 1606-7 reminds us. Also, rainfall tends to be high. Furthermore, the Bristol Channel is noted for one of the greatest tidal rises in Europe. The rhynes play their traditional part in draining and guarding the land, aided by such natural rivers as the Brue and Parrett, supplemented by important waterways like Huntspill River, a wide sweep from the coast running well inland, as if a giant knife had slashed across the lowlands in two parallel strokes, cleaving a great gash filled with shining water.

Most lanes across the moors, running as straight as everything else in this vast open-air geometry book, are bordered on both sides by narrower ditches separating the fields, in place of hedges; it is not unknown for the occasional driver after dark not, as city motorists do, attempting to climb a lamp-post, but taking a ducking in a roadside dyke. Such accidents sometimes result in drownings, as local inquest reports show even now. Wives awaiting overdue husbands known to be driving across the moors feel an apprehension quite unfamiliar to wives of city men kept late at the office. They are descendants of travellers' wives of centuries before, when the dark eerie moors with their unexpected bogs and ditches claimed occasional victims; an ancient Somerset wassail song includes the lines:

O master and mistress, a-sitting by the fire,
Pray think upon poor travellers, a-travelling in the mire.

At least three human occupations have traditionally been followed on the moors: dairying and other farming; peat digging; and willow growing. The latter fall into two groups, the ubiquitous truncated pollarded willows, used for stakes, sticks, basketry and other wooden objects, and the less well-known but interesting cricket-bat willow. Cricket-bat willows are fussy creatures, demanding careful siting; they like running water nearby but the soil must also be well drained and, in times of flood, the water must drain off quickly. True marshland of sedges and rushes, where irises and thick meadowsweet grow, is too damp. A site showing nettles, the clinging goose-grass and cow-parsley may suit its taste. Finding a suitable home for cricket-bat willows is like satisfying a disgruntled maiden aunt on a housing estate, where every home has something somewhere to raise disapproval. Even when all its whims have been satisfied, only parts of the tree are used for cricket bats. Cricket-bat willows played an unexpected part in protecting the solvency of one of Somerset's best known factories during the great Depression; the beautiful willows in the factory grounds were sold to a sports manufacturer for a satisfactory sum when money was needed most.

Peat-cutting is another localised occupation, for horticultural purposes rather than heating nowadays. Peat, sometimes also called turf, is composed of waterlogged decaying vegetable matter, being in fact coal in its infancy. As well as being useful fuel, it can be dug back into the soil elsewhere, improving the moisture-retaining property of dry soils. It is also a plant nutrient.

Turbary is the accepted title for peat-giving land, and the cut lumps are usually called turf or turves. The spade remains the most useful implement for bringing up the flat rectangular blocks of dark wet peat. These are then set to dry in humped mounds or ruckles, with spaces left between turves to allow the passage of air for drying. The turbary lands are easily recognisable by the dark brown mounds of drying peat. The long trenches from which fresh peat has been taken often fill with water, showing how much ground-water still lies under this damp outpost of ancient England; here again Holland comes to mind, where the spade frequently meets water only a few feet down when digging in the polderlands.

Shapwick, Westhay and Godney are among the chief peat-giving areas. Even now the business has its own technical language, from processing to final sale. Time was when turves were delivered cut in the shape of lawn turves, at so much a load, but nowadays they come in large polythene bags. A fire of Somerset peat gives out a distinctive sweet scent, especially when mixed with logs and a little coal. For centuries it was a common fuel; as recently as the war, peat was a godsend as a supplement to strictly rationed coal. Today its most important function is horticultural, as a fertiliser and compost among many and various uses. So far I have never seen it used as roofing, as was done in Norway; many older barns and outhouses sprout a soft covering of grass on their ancient peat roofs, complete with blue harebells in July.

As is well known, peat has a preservative property towards buried historic relics, rather as lava has preserved Pompeii and Hurculaneum. Unlike most soils, it does not allow the complete decay of wooden objects, to the joy of archaeologists. The lake villages at Meare and Godney are the classic examples of wood being kept intact in peat, but there are also Neolithic and Bronze Age roadways of timber, ancient predecessors of the duckboard method of traversing marshy or muddy land. Nearly twenty such trackways have been found up to the time of writing; scientific tests date them to about 3,000 years before Christ.

Dairying is the chief moorland occupation, and the Pawlett Hams are considered the finest cattle-rearing land in all this great area of nutritious grazing. The Hams, towards the seaward side of the moors, consist of thousands of acres of the finest pastureland in Somerset, and were once partly the property of John of Gaunt; Gaunt's Farm appears on the current Ordnance map of the lowlands.

Watching a herd of cows eating its way from tussock to tussock of lush moorland grass, twitching their tails as they move, is a wonderful cure for the stresses and strains of city life. Unfortunately it does not appear in the British Pharmacopoeia. A prescription for "one week spent watching one herd of cows somewhere between Meare and nowhere, plus one return fare and seven days' farmhouse lodging" might have as good an effect on some patients as many a tranquilliser on the National Health. Cattle dotted all over the vast flat miles of moorland resemble a pattern of coloured spots on a thick-pile green carpet. Towards milking time they instinctively turn farmwards, plodding in long files like armies on the march as do the cow processions on Sedgemoor. A regiment of ponderous bodies slowly walking across a causeway, silhouetted against the bright sky, is a peculiarly lowland sight, while on the quiet lanes a lorry load of rattling milk-churns is more likely to be encountered than a stream of cars.

Meare, the only sizeable place, might be called the capital of the central moors, set on what was a low islet in the heart of the kingdom of the ancient waters. The Mere from which its name derives, five miles in circumference in Elizabeth I's day, survived as late as the 18th century, long after the marshes and waters around it had gone. In winter flood Meare Pool covered as much as 500 acres; one cannot but regret its passing; not only must it have been a very lovely sheet of water, teeming with fish and sailed by swans and wildfowl, but it must also have given a good idea what the country as a whole looked like when all was lakeland.

The most interesting survival of Meare's fishing days is the Abbot's Fish House, built six centuries ago, when Meare supplied the great monastery of Glastonbury. The Abbot's steward, head of the fisheries, lived on the upper floor, while tackle was stored below. Constructed of stone and massive timbers, the Fish House, built in a chapel-like style, presents a mellow picture when seen in golden sunshine across meadows bright with even more golden buttercups. It stands at the point marking the lake shore, as can be discerned in the upward shelving of the land from the ocean of wind-whispering grasses and rushes around it.

Fishing at Meare was a highly organised and profitable business in Glastonbury's heyday, fish being required on Fridays, fast-days, and during Lent when meat was not allowed to be eaten. About 5,000 eels alone were landed from Meare Pool in an average year. Today's Ordnance maps show numerous placenames perpetuating the ancient fisheries: Fishpond Farm, Decoy Pool Farm, Withy Farm (withies are a form of reed used in basket making), while the name Meare Pool actually appears on the map, over what is now pastureland, where the Pool formerly lay.

The last days of Glastonbury were its great days, when the monastery was at the height of its power, richness, and beauty. Its Abbots had assumed an appropriate authority and wealth, and did not confine themselves to the piety of a monastic cell; they steadily acquired a string of country houses in addition to what was by then a regal lodging within the Abbey itself. From these rural seats they enjoyed the invigorating country air, or indulged in such unecclesiastical sports as shooting. During the 14th century the current Abbot added the manor house of Meare, communicating with the Abbey by barge. Guests likewise were carried over the waters of the beautiful wind-brushed lake. It must have been a pleasant spot in summer, where fruit ripened and cattle waxed sleek, though cut off by floods in winter.

Meare remembers a saint with four names, all beginning with B, and is famous for the discovery of the lake villages where men lived among the spreading lakes of pre-Christian Somerset. What a varied catalogue of interest is centred on an apparently ordinary village in the heart of a uniformly flat plain. Meare does not feature in coach-tour itineraries, but for the visitor with ears to listen to tales of the past – the very, very distant past – and imagination enough to visualise what he hears, a trip to Meare on a rattling country bus can be extremely rewarding, even though there is little on the outward surface, apart from the Fish House, to bear witness of its interesting history.

Two major saints are remembered in the Somerset lowlands, Dunstan and Patrick, but Meare boasts a third, a minor but intriguing figure said to have followed St. Patrick when he came in old age to Glastonbury, there to retire in company with a few holy hermits, and there to die, as Glastonbury tradition tells. The third saint was Bennings, a friend of St. Patrick who was divinely inspired to follow him from Ireland; the staff he carried was to burst into foliage where he was to build his own hermit's cell, which miracle materialised at Meare. There Bennings settled, walking all the way to Glastonbury daily – presumably over some ancient causeway above the mire – to hear Mass. He was eventually buried at Meare in the 5th century. An Abbot of Glastonbury had the bones exhumed for re-burial in a new church built in his name. First Bennings' remains were enclosed in a gold cloth container, prayed over by monks for eight weeks, before the translation by boat to the new church at Glastonbury. Like all good legends, that of Bennings has a miraculous twist; at the final Benediction, all the sick present were cured. Later the church of St. Bennings or Benignus was rededicated to St. Bennet or Benedict: so says one version. Another holds that he was buried in the Abbey itself, the other marking the resting place of the body en route from Meare, and that the Church of St. Bennings, Bennet, Benignus, or Benedict is one and the same: you pays your money and you takes your legendary pick.

Before any of these saints, before the coming of Christianity itself, a group of men and women were living in the weird watery wilderness near where Meare and Godney now stand; the discovery of the sites of their strange villages is one of the great archaeological narratives of our time. During the 19th century, exceptionally severe droughts lowered the level of the Swiss lakes as had never been seen within living memory; hitherto water-covered marsh lay exposed, and the people decided to reclaim it permanently. Work on the reclamation projects uncovered something completely unexpected: evidence of human habitation on what was normally the lakes' beds. The Somerset antiquarian Arthur Bulleid saw a resemblance to the Somerset moors which had also once been a lake's bed: if men had lived among the reedy fringes of the Swiss lakes, had there been similar settlements in Somerset? None knew better than Bulleid the geography of the Somerset plains, how they had once lain under water. Thenceforth his archaeologist's eye was alert for any telltale signs.

One day Bulleid spotted some low mounds, alien to their dead-level setting, where ditch diggers were working. Had they ever noticed anything unusual about the mounds, he enquired. Ornamented pottery had indeed been unearthed, they confirmed; Bulleid was on the trail of the most exciting discovery in the county. Soon the site of a second lake-village was found; careful digging over many years unearthed a picture of life in primitive huts built on skilful foundations, inhabited by simple people who had surprising skill in their hands and highly creative artistic minds, as the jewellery and ornamented pottery they left tells. The villages were constructed on artificial "islands" made from heavy baulks of timber sunk into the lake floor and built up to above water level, surrounded by protective stockades of closely-spaced wooden stakes. Some of the timber when discovered, thanks to the preserving quality of the peat, still showed axe marks, as fresh as when first cut, though they lost this newness quickly on exposure to the air. On the islands many small round huts were built; archaeological artists' representations suggest buildings reminiscent of the jungle rather than cool Somerset, built of mud and wattle with hayrick-shaped straw roofs. The floors were of clay, whose weight often sank down; the answer was a new floor above the old – as many as ten floors have been found one above the other in a single dwelling. Many had stone hearths; the stone must have been rowed from the Mendips or Poldens, for certainly none was available locally. A causeway linked the villages with drier ground, as excavations have revealed. Experts disagree, as experts will, on the period during which the villages were occupied, but the average guess seems to be from about 300 B.C. until well into the Roman occupation of Britain.

Why were the villages finally abandoned? We shall never rightly know. Some speculate that the inhabitants were lured elsewhere to the civilised life of Romanised Somerset; others that one flood, mightier than those periodically sweeping the swamplands, destroyed it; others prefer a more gruesome end, with enemies surprising the inhabitants by night in a bloody massacre. The more mundane flood theory, however, seems most feasible if less spectacular.

To casual observers the lake-village sites show little above ground. The interesting finds are mainly in the Tribunal museum at Glastonbury, well classified, where the curators are pleased to give a wealth of information to genuinely interested visitors. The wooden pieces are rarest; wood on ancient sites has normally rotted entirely, but in Somerset the peat has preserved some amazing things, including a large dug-out canoe shaped from a hollowed out tree trunk, in which the marsh-men paddled about their watery world; it is over five metres long, and for its age in remarkable condition. These supposedly primitive people had an almost geometrical artistic skill, decorating their pottery with intricate and delicately cut designs of considerable beauty and fineness of detail; we today would be far from ashamed to own some of these beautifully decorated pots of over 2,000 year ago. Bone weaving combs, too, are of delicate ornamentation and carefully aligned teeth, and there is a collection of truly beautiful coloured beads and rings, including a ring of shining black jet. There are common domestic articles of wood and bone: a needle with a narrow eye; a pair of tweezers, and spinning whorls. All these and more were dug from the flat unassuming moors of Meare and Godney.

Although the finds at Meare and Godney rank with the major archaeological discoveries of the past century, such villages were apparently not unique to the Somerset fens. Lake settlements have also been unearthed in England's other great fenland area, East Anglia, an interesting parallel study, including the wooden piles, shaped flints, and various weapons from a site near Braintree in Essex.

There are few villages actually on the moors, apart from Meare, Westhay and Godney; the others tend to circle the moor, almost touching the first contours of the Polden, Wedmore or West Pennard hillsides. One of these, Baltonsborough, may appear, quite erroneously, as a rather nondescript place; even local people tend to think it obscure and "Baltonsboroughites" country bumpkins compared with the residents of Street and Glastonbury. Actually, it has two great distinctions, being the birthplace of Dunstan, Somerset's favourite saint, and the home of one of the most exotic plants of the steaming tropical jungles, cultivated on a serious scale in supposedly humble Baltonsborough.

St. Dunstan was born at Baltonsborough and educated by the monks of Glastonbury; eventually be returned to the Abbey in about A.D. 945 as its ruling Abbot, and began one of the several reconstructions leading to its establishment as one of the premier foundations in all England. Dunstan rose even higher in the Church; ultimately the boy from Baltonsborough became Archbishop of Canterbury. Scanty remains of Dunstan's buildings at Glastonbury still survive, with a legend attached as one might expect of this legendary place; an ancient record tells that as a youth Dunstan was visited by an angel who showed him in a dream the buildings of a great monastery, telling him that he would one day see that Abbey built, and become its Abbot. Dunstan remains a local saint, whose erudition and work for his people are not forgotten. Needless to say, Baltonsborough church is dedicated to him. During the last 25 years the extent of Dunstan's work at Glastonbury, domestic as well as ecclesiastical, has been ascertained by excavations, adding greatly to available information on the earlier monasteries on the present Abbey's site.

Baltonsborough is not a village one would associate with the tropics, but it is noted for nurseries rearing an amazing variety of glorious orchids in every colour of the spectrum. One of the first stands met by patrons of the Chelsea Flower Show may well be a display of these hypnotically beautiful flowers, labelled "Baltonsborough, near Glastonbury, Somerset". The place of origin mystifies show buyers more than the plants themselves; "Where on earth is Baltonsborough?" I heard more than one exclaim last year. The nurseries claim to keep about 100,000 of the exotic plants in stock at any one time, and the glasshouses cover two acres. Even their names take one on a trip into a tropical fantasy: Bali, Korsokobb, Anacapa, Euphrates, Esmeralda.

Yes, there is a lot more to the central moorlands than an endless succession of dead flat fields and grazing cattle. They have a beauty that insinuates itself into the hearts of those who know them, not flaunting itself on the eye as do the Mendip gorges, but quietly piercing deep into the affections. To those who know the moors, their moods, and something of their industries, ways of life, and history, this is the most loved part of Somerset.

The Isle of Wedmore
Danes and Dairymaids

6

WHOEVER has spent a holiday on the Somerset coast, enlivened by trips to the usual sightseers' goals, but who has not also driven inland to the moors and the ancient islands can hardly claim to have seen the county's full face. Admittedly, many do cross the plains via the Isle of Wedmore, but only because this is a convenient cross-country route from the sands of Burnham to Wells, seeing Wedmore itself as worth no more than a passing glance.

Likewise, the narrow moorland strip between Wedmore and the Mendips is virtually on the doorstep of one of England's most celebrated sights, Cheddar: but who has heard of Cheddar Moor, much less stepped upon it?

These two areas, the Isle of Wedmore and the moors set between it and the Mendips, are not tourist districts; they are the farmers' Somerset, historic but unassuming agricultural lands with a character all their own.

Immediately west of Wells are a series of rounded and oblong outliers, small distinctly separated hills rising from the plains; it needs little imagination to realise that they were once islands, as was the longer and broader Isle of Wedmore continuing the chain westwards. Nor is the imagination overtaxed in picturing the possible nature of the intervening moorlands; hemmed in from the main Somerset fenlands by Wedmore, they must surely have been chiefly marshy backwaters and mire, with stretches of clearer water at the broadest parts. Perhaps in winter, when water off the hills and tides from the Bristol Channel combined to raise the overall level of the main Somerset lakeland, this stretch, too, was all open water, but only mud, fen and mire in summer. This is of course but surmise, remembering that the famous lake-villages were apparently surrounded by water up to about 3ft. deep at times, but at other times were fringed only by marshes, as the discovery both of a causeway link with dryer ground and also of dug-out boats for use on open water implies. Picturing the landscape's likely nature at any given point is a fascinating Somerset pastime.

The best way to turn imagination into a semblance of reality is to view the Isle of Wedmore across Axbridge reservoir. There is no need to trespass to get close to the lake; the aspect from the main Axbridge-Wells road or some of the lanes leading off it in the lake direction is quite sufficient to give a picture of Wedmore as it may have appeared during winter high water. Refreshing breezes froth the lake into a sweep of lapping wavelets, making it seem larger than its mile or so across, the Isle forming a long low ridge of dry land beyond; was this our ancestors' impression of the Isle of Wedmore?

Note the title, Isle of Wedmore: it is one of the few ancient islands retaining that designation in this century. It might be considered to begin at Theale and reach its broadest point around Wedmore itself, before turning in a more northerly direction to merge finally into the coastal plain at Weare and Badgworth. There is the feeling of an island about it, cut off from the show-places by that protecting area of moors which gives the casual traveller the erroneous impression that nothing of distinction lies beyond it to justify an exploratory detour. In reality, Wedmore is worth a visit, if only to sample the quality of agricultural, uncommercialised Somerset.

King Alfred is understood to have had a palace there; the massive remains of an obviously important structure found near the hamlet of Mudgley may possibly be a part. King Ine of the Saxons is also believed to have maintained an establishment there, while supervising one of the several rebuildings; of Glastonbury Abbey, several miles away across the marshes; possibly it was the same building.

It was to Alfred's Wedmore palace that Guthrum the Dane came to sign the peace treaty which is the sole reason for Wedmore's appearing in the history books. A.D. 878 saw the ending of years of feuding between the two parties, one set upon acquiring the portions of southern England not yet under his power, the other equally determined to prevent the subjugation of Wessex to the Danes, even though they had already over-run at least three other kingdoms. This Alfred did at Ethandune, following which the historic Peace of Wedmore was made. By this treaty the bounds of Wessex and the Danelaw were defined: "Let the bounds of our dominion stretch to the River Thames, and from thence to the water of the Lea, even unto the head of the same water, and thence straight unto Bedford, and finally along by the River Ouse, let them end at Watling Street".

Few invaders can have been more confident than the Danes of ultimate victory, having gained so much already, but Alfred was not easily defeated. All the more determined to succeed in yet another campaign, he assembled his army at Athelney, briefed them for an all-out assault on the enemy, met him, and at long last overcame him; the site of Ethandune is doubtful, both Edington, Somerset and Edington, Wiltshire, claiming to be the place; the outcome was more certain: victory for Alfred.

Alfred insisted on more than a peace pact with Guthrum the Dane; he also required him to embrace the faith he himself believed. As a Christian king he shunned the usual slaughter of prisoners following a battle; instead Guthrum and about three score of his men were baptised, Alfred sponsoring the man he had defeated. By a happy chance the 1,000th anniversary of the Peace of Wedmore fell during the reign of the Edward who became known as The Peacemaker: a simple reminder in Wedmore church notes: "Alfred the King at Wedmore made peace. Death of Alfred 901 – Edward the Seventh 1901". Thereafter Wedmore bowed out of all but local history, giving itself to farming, especially to dairying; a single day of history-making was followed by a thousand years when the dairy-maid was of more consequence than the Dane.

Wedmore Town exudes something of the dignity of an island capital in its mellow and gracious properties, and part of it is still given the high-sounding title, The Borough. It is an interchange point for buses meeting from cross-country routes, has several inns, a sprinkling of Non-conformist churches, and examples of several periods of domestic building. The parish church is imposing, partly of the 12th and 14th centuries, but mainly dating from the immensely rich period of the Somerset Perpendicular. Like St. John's at Glastonbury it commemorates in glass some highlights of local history, including Alfred making peace with the Danes, and the famous burning of the cakes.

Churches may appeal to the architecturally uninformed casual visitor only in the guise of a quick look around; treasure-trove, on the other hand, is beloved of all. The treasure of Wedmore may be mentioned in a few lines of a guide-book, but has a much more vivid impact from the lips of a local tale-teller, even though he or she does embroider it a little. One night in the 11th century, during some threatened upheaval or conflict, an unknown man came to the churchyard carrying his life's nest-egg, a jar of coins, to hide it in what seemed the safest temporary bank. He never returned, presumably having died in whatever trouble it was that prompted him to provide for a future he was not destined to see. So well did he conceal his hoard that his wealth lay undiscovered for no less than 800 years, its original monetary value transferred into a much higher historic worth. Now the anonymous saver's coins, a priceless treasure of the reigns of Canute and Harold among others, repose in the British Museum.

A little-known local benefactor earned a niche in medical history, at a time when mental affliction was treated like a crime instead of an illness, the day of the horrors of Bedlam as so vividly portrayed by Hogarth in 'The Rake's Progress'. John Westover inaugurated a small private practice among mental cases of the 17th century, building a solid stone house for their treatment in this restful West Country village, anticipating the modern acceptance of country life and surroundings as of therapeutic value in psychiatric treatment. Lucky were the sufferers from mental disturbance of central Somerset, who had this almost unsung pioneer doctor to thank for treatment looking towards today's methods.

Hannah More, the vigorous social reformer, on the other hand found Wedmore disturbing to her high-principled soul, when her efforts to start a little school met with hostility from local farmers. "Shocking" and "depraved" were but two of the epithets the well-meaning lady levelled at the place.

Today the Isle manages to stand a little apart from the pace of the contemporary scene, an excellent reason for savouring its secluded villages and fine viewpoints. There are splendid panoramas of the Mendip Hills from the northern flanks of the island, rarely extolled in the briefer guide-books but well worth discovering and lingering over. Why not, indeed, give Cheddar a miss for one day, devoting it instead to exploring Wedmore's villages and letting the pastoral atmosphere do more for the soul than will trudging around with chattering guided parties?

Chapel Allerton is in what might be called Wedmore's windmill belt, having the remains of one of several mills built to catch the driving force of the brisk breezes off the open moors below. Some have gone, some have been converted into unusual homes, and another, at Ashton, has been restored, though not to working order, as an example of the windmills of the Isle.

Then there is Stone Allerton, whose Manor Farm of 1772 marks the site of an even older manor. From the edge of the Isle it looks out across the blue-green flatness of the moors to the dominating landmark of Brent Knoll, a rural retreat of narrow lanes where a tractor ramming a dung-cart is newsworthy of local newspaper reportage. All around are fields, and attractive old cottages whose characters have not been destroyed by discreet necessary modernisation, such as turning a bedroom into a bathroom to replace the old outside closet with tin bucket.

Weare is one of the last villages, where the northern flank of the Isle runs down towards the moors. Strange though it seems now, it was once important enough to be a Borough. Mark poses a geographical problem for the writer: does it belong to the moors, together with the Mark Causeway whose name recalls the marshland causeways of old, or is it the last outpost of Wedmore? The parish embraces both, extending onto the Isle's lower slopes. Mark was once favoured by the powerful Abbots of Glastonbury, as a country retreat, who visited their manor there by barge. The patronage of Abbots of one of England's richest Abbeys gave Mark a reflected importance, but the Abbey's downfall did not destroy it; there was still a profitable income from sheep rearing, as its fine "wool church" reflects. Among its many carved figures are saints, bishops, angels, King Alfred, and Guthrum. This motley collection continues into our own century, with Edward VII and his beautiful Queen Alexandra.

A day spent exploring the Isle of Wedmore, bigger than it looks, is one of the best ways to get into the skin of country life. Best of all, have a glass of scrumpy cider in a village inn while emulating the three wise monkeys – hear all, see all, say nowt. Listen instead to the babble of local voices: "G'won with 'ee, that … doan't know what 'ee'm talking of"; of a neighbour's wife: "Git on! She bain't no chicken! Fifty yurr if she be a day". You may hear picturesque epithets: "As fat as an old fool", or "Ee be all of a dizz-wazz, mazez as a sheep"; in annoyance: "I never 'eard sich sass in all my born days", or in contempt: "Lazy? 'Ee bain't done a stroke of work since Currsmass". And, of course, the inevitable bar-room joker: "Yurr! Have 'ee 'eard this 'un?". Such is the natural speech of the country, not stage Zummerzet. This is not to say that West Country speech should not be used to put over a story in an appealing way, without the distortion of a comedy turn, gripping the ear by its sheer attraction. A good example is the series of Biblical episodes retold in West Country by that supreme character actor, Bernard Miles, on an early morning radio programme. Listening, it is easy to picture an old farmer in his rocking chair, smelling subtly of baccy and pigsty, telling his grandchildren about Palm Sunday or Easter, without the slightest irreverence but an outstanding charm and humour. Sit back, then, in a village bar; drink, listen, and remember something the coach parties miss while racing through Cheddar, Wells and Glastonbury in one day, imagining they have, as our friends from across the Atlantic put it, "done Somerset".

Perhaps second only to local speech is local weather forecasting, to the interested stranger. It is an important skill where the weather governs anything from haymaking to potato lifting; it is no use setting out to cut a hay field in dazzling sunshine, if rain is to creep up an hour later. Farmers know the signs. They have to. I remember setting out once in pouring rain with a West Country man, though rain appeared to have set in for the day if not the week. "Don't 'ee worry; 'ee'l be out by three", he forecast. At twenty to three we still drove through lashing rain and then ... what was that lighter patch over the hills? Was that the sun peering through? It was. And the time? Four minutes to three. Weather signs if read and understood correctly are a remarkably reliable guide for the immediate locality; leaves blowing persistently backwards to show their undersides mean approaching rain, as do birds flying low over the ground, clouds like a flock of sheep across the sky, or cats waking from the normal feline stupor to become unusually excited and playful, careering up trees or chasing nothing with ears flung back and eyes sparkling. A herd of cows noticeably face in the same direction, showing the wind's quarter. Raindrops clinging to windows and windscreens after the rain has stopped mean more to come; the air is too moist for the drops to evaporate. Rheumatic pain increased, often means rain – "I can feel it in my bones", as they say. Strangely, the pain comes while the weather is yet fine, and if note is taken will probably be found to set in at the same time as the barometer begins to fall; bones and barometers sense the change together; the pain will often vanish when the rain arrives, again with the turn of the mercury, foretelling an end to the present dampness.

The addition of some locally gleaned weather lore enables one to form a pretty accurate forecast in a different locality, or even a different country. In the Alps, for instance, a bridal wreath of mist around one peak while certain others are clear denotes a fine day, but if both are clear it may mean a fine morning and an afternoon deterioration. On many a holiday I have become the party's unofficial weather forecaster; from Switzerland to the Tyrol, from Spain to Norway, I have had my estimates borne out; an observant eye and the handed-down age-old lore of the sky rarely fail.

Wedmore must have been a haven of good grazing far back in early history when it was a true island of well-drained land in the fens. For centuries the dairy-maid was as important in her own field as were the farmer and the cowherd. Doubtless the availability of satisfactory grazing was responsible for the growth of human settlements on the Isle, where men could rear cattle and make a living above the unhealthy mists or vapours of the marshlands.

Country life is leisurely – on the surface. In reality the work is hard and demanding, with no respect for wet feet, aching muscles, or the Sunday lie-in. The land is a hard master, and cows are harder mistresses; they must be milked on a glorious morning, and at the same hour in snowy January twilight; they have a habit of calving in the middle of the night, or on a Bank Holiday; they want feeding and watering, even the morning after a cider-swigging night before, when the cowman is sickening for flu, or the wife has just produced twins. A couple of farmhands "argifying" over a wall in morning sunshine makes the work and hours of a London office seem hard, but in practice they have completed their smelly chores before the average city man has even got out of bed: yes, even in a snowstorm. As an old farmer remarked: "Cows bain't your'n; you belongs to them". The hours when visitors drive through the country, seeing only the interludes giving an impression of a permanent siesta, are usually those between the morning milking and mucking-out, and the later milking and feeding – unless, of course, something else crops up, such as haymaking, harvesting, strawberry picking, fruit packing, planting out, bale heaving, shed repairing, ditch clearing, or sundry other farm jobs. So much for the easy-going life down on the farm.

Burnham and the Coastal Levels
Four B's and the Severn Sea

THREE neighbouring resorts strung along the edge of the Severn Sea, or Bristol Channel, and a lone hill second only to Glastonbury Tor as a landmark have one thing in common: their names all begin with B. They are Burnham, Berrow, Brean and Brent Knoll.

Burnham-on-Sea, biggest of these Severn Sea resorts, sprang from a hamlet mentioned in King Alfred's will as worth £4; in the 18th century it was a small impoverished village. Not until the invention, if that is the right word, of the seaside holiday in Georgian and Victorian times did Burnham begin to develop into a sedate little watering place. As late as the Second World War it was known chiefly to West Country people as a popular venue for family outings and for organised children's excursions by the deeply lamented Somerset and Dorset Railway from Glastonbury. Burnham's wide sands and tangy breezes drew families from all over the Channel hinterland, despite the fact that for a fair slice of the day it was often a seaside without the sea.

With the advent of free-and-easy caravan and camping holidays, now a recognised and highly profitable part of the holiday industry throughout Europe, Burnham came to wider life. Parents, saddled with a brood of infants too unrestrained to be taken to an hotel, began to take more and more to the relaxed informal atmosphere of camping on properly organised sites with necessary amenities, yet without personal restrictions. Burnham, Brean and Berrow already had a sprinkling of chalets and caravan parks along the breezy dunes; they have grown into a series of informal holiday sites, known to thousands who before the war had never heard of Burnham. The whole area offers an unusually wide selection of caravan parks, chalets, and larger holiday camps. In addition, Burnham has more holiday flats than any other seaside resort I know, many on the seafront itself where would usually be only hotels; there families can enjoy the easy going do-it-yourself type of relaxation in a temporary home of their own.

A child's idea of Heaven the beach on a fine day may be, as much so now as during the war or in Victoria's reign. The beach is Burnham's all: mile on mile of firm tide-washed sands; sandcastle digging; a paddling pool of sea water left by the last tide; playing among the dunes where strange rush-like grasses poke through the sands like stiff green spikes; ball games on the sands; walking out to the unusual Lighthouse On Legs; and the excitement of waiting for the tide to come in. And it is a thrill, for the sea retreats to a thin shining ribbon on the horizon where the luring islands of Steep Holme and Flat Holm guard the Channel. For a few hours miles of glistening mud and sand have been exposed. But go gift buying in the shopping streets parallel with the Esplanade, take a meal and a look at the church, and when you come back – there is the sea. It has returned as fast as it went. Those living near enough to go late in the day let the tide rather than the hour rule their departure; it is nothing unusual for a relative to knock on the door as far inland as Street at 6 p.m., saying "Be 'ee coming to Burnham? The tide will be in". Then there is the drive back across the midnight-blue dusky moors, hearing such tales as that of Swayne and his leaps in Loxley Woods, or of the ghosts of Monmouth's slain, wandering on Sedgemoor.

Evening at Burnham also shows the fine views from its Esplanade at their best, tide or no tide. Steep Holme and Flat Holm stand out against the lowering sun, and beyond them the Welsh mountains become sharper as the shadows fall into the valleys. Across the Parrett estuary a long silent coast runs for miles with the blue-grey Quantocks and the borders of Devon as backcloth. This lonely coast of sand-dunes and crying sea birds has a not entirely detrimental contemporary landmark, the nuclear power station at Hinckley Point. Close up it may be bare and functional, but from a distance it adds perspective to the unbroken coastline, its square bulk not unlike that of a Norman castle keep in the dusk.

The sands are apparently the be-all and end-all of Burnham, but on second thoughts it has much to offer the open-air minded adult. Sailing, despite the shortness of the possible launching period on each tide, is popular; perhaps the challenge to good seamanship of the tricky tides, treacherous banks, and estuary currents attracts the true sportsman to this coast.

Angling is the top adult activity, with the choice of sea, lake or river within the one locality. At high tide there may be fishing from the sea wall for plaice, cod, whiting and squirming eels. There are three rivers at hand, the Brue, Parrett and Huntspill. The Huntspill has been the setting for All-England championships several times, speaking for itself of the area's appeal to anglers. The famous Chew Valley lake is a moderate drive inland, beyond the Mendips.

Burnham's seafront can by no stretch of the imagination be called spectacular; it is a very modest old-fashioned little town, in pleasant contrast to the big English resorts with their standardised rows of hotels and their piers. Like the rest of Burnham the old church, just off the seafront behind a pleasant sunken garden, is unassuming from the outside. Its most noticeable feature is the leaning tower, the result of its being built upon sand; local lore says that in winter winds the leaning tower invokes hideous shrieks and moans like the soundtrack of a horror film.

Inside the church, the mantle of modesty is cast aside, revealing a completely unexpected treasure; this quiet seaside church possesses a large part of the glorious reredos whose travels took it from a royal palace to Westminster Abbey before it found a home here. How did such a priceless piece, the handiwork of Inigo Jones and Grinling Gibbons, among others, come to rest in Burnham? It so happened that a former vicar of Burnham became Bishop of Rochester in Kent, a post at that time linked with the Deanery of Westminster. During a refurbishing of the Abbey for George IV's coronation, the huge reredos was replaced by work in the more fashionable Gothic manner, cast off like a piece of unwanted furniture. The Bishop, remembering his old parish church, acquired the sculpture that had adorned first Whitehall Palace and then the Abbey, for Burnham. It was of necessity broken up, scattered around the church. A specially fine group of angels and cherubs reposes under the tower.

Church and lighthouses have historic connections. A Burnham curate with some knowledge of geology once dug a number of wells, hoping to make the town a spa when such places were at the height of fashion. He also owned a lighthouse, charging toll to ships using its services, with which to finance his well-boring operations. It is said that originally a fisherman's wife, anxious for her husband on a stormy night, lit a candle at the window to guide him in. Other sailors, seeing the life-saving value of the light, paid her to maintain it. The local sexton, sensing a good thing, took the right from her for £5, transferring the light to the church tower. Soon after, the canny curate in turn bought him out for £20, and forthwith erected a new building on the dunes. When the present lighthouse replaced it, he was able to sell his rights for over £13,000. Today Burnham has the High Lighthouse, on land, and the curious Lighthouse On Legs, on the sands. That strange little structure surmounts the local coat of arms, which include the sun, the waves of the sea, and three cows' heads as a reminder that Burnham was once a farming village.

Plenty of little human-interest stories lie behind the modern scene, as any local resident will tell. I came across a charming tale while writing this chapter, of a cat-loving man of earlier days who regularly trundled a barrow loaded with fish through the coastal towns, stopping at cat owners' doors to thrust fish wrapped in newspaper through the letter boxes. Needless to say, he was followed by a collection of local moggies, like a fish-dispensing Pied Piper.

The coast held danger for mariners for centuries; it still has veiled menace, towards unaware young paddlers too immersed in play to notice the quickly incoming tide. I recall several outings being shadowed by unnecessary drownings while mothers gossiped. This is not to condemn Burnham beach as a children's playground – far from it – but simply to draw attention to the fact that on coasts where the tide retreats far but returns fast, such as the Bristol Channel and Thames Estuary, small children need watching. In one respect this is safer than certain South Coast beaches, where sudden drops in the level of the shingle, disguised by water, mean that paddlers may be in inches of water one moment and out of their depth the next; there are no such traps at Burnham where the sands shelve so gently as to look almost level.

There is a clearly defined line between the playground sands and the oozing flats left by the tide; those expanses of damp mud are sometimes called quicksands, but are really only ordinary tidal mud of a specially squelchy character. The mud and sandbanks continually shift with tides and currents, and were a notorious ships' graveyard before the advent of lighthouses and modern navigational aids.

The shifting banks of the Parrett estuary have been kept clear by small dredgers. Much older, and still remembered by longstanding residents, were the Parrett flatners, distinctive flat-bottomed fishing vessels designed to safely cross the shallow estuary. They were of very ancient origin, possibly having an ancestry reaching as far back as Viking days. The rather crude design remained almost constant throughout the flatner's history; in appearance, it was not unlike a dorey. It was unique to the Parrett coast, able to slip across shallow waters only a foot or two deep where other craft would have grounded.

Seawards from Burnham Esplanade, the fine outlook is dominated by Steep Holme and Flat Holm, beckoning with the strange compelling lure of all islands. Motor boats can take visitors to Flat Holm from Weston-super-Mare in summer if both weather and tide are favourable; the trip is worth doing for the Crusoe experience of being on a lonely isle having only a lighthouse and one cottage, halfway between England and Wales.

Steep Holme, geographically a last outpost of the Mendip massif, is very different, a rounded rocky mass of sheer cliffs. It is a famous bird sanctuary, but not accessible to the general public. Keen botanists and ornithologists can land with special permission – and they have to be keen to risk being marooned on this inhospitable uninhabited island armed only with binoculars, cameras and sleeping bags. If wind, weather or tide change unexpectedly for the worse, picking up from Steep Holme ranges from the dangerous to the impossible, leaving the explorers with more time for bird-watching than they bargained for.

Viking ships once used Steep Holme as a base for raiding the undefended coast. According to legend one raid ended in disaster for the warriors, thanks to the most helpless of the people who fled before them, a crippled woman whose legs could not carry her fast enough. Instead she hid behind a rock, watching the plunderers creep away. While they were gone the old lady hobbled to the unattended boats, loosed their moorings, and left them to drift and sink. The returning raiders, bereft of their boats, were slaughtered by the rest of the villagers.

Burnham, thanks to the combination of geographical aspect in relation to the sun plus its shining mudbanks, has a name for spectacular sunsets, a distinction it shares with Weston-super-Mare. Accentuated by the colour-catching tidal flats the evening sky often blazes like fire. Given a camera with a sufficiently deep lenshood one can record a complete sequence from the first pink flush, through the brilliant reds and golds of sunset, to the final afterglow as the first lamps are lit. During an eruption of Vesuvius some years ago, when volcanic ash particles floating in the air produced wonderful sunsets all over Europe, Burnham's already lavish spectacles were of an unforgettable glory, a blend of fiery reds with orange, palest green and turquoise, opal and salmon. A painter attempting to record them would have been accused of hopeless exaggeration.

All the same, painters do attempt to capture the evening's colouring over the Severn Sea. I have been told several times that Turner, to whom the play of light, colour and atmosphere were so beloved, came to Burnham to paint its famous sunsets, though the London galleries seem not to be aware of the works' titles or whereabouts. It is, however, documented that Turner made a sketching tour of Somerset in 1811. A sketchbook of around 1799, known to the Tate Gallery, shows a list of places the painter presumably intended to visit, including Bridgwater, Athelney, Wells and Glastonbury. A copy of Coltman's "British Itinerary" likewise has a list of placenames, several of them on the north Devon coast plus Minehead and Watchet in Somerset, and Weston. The latter is crossed out: had Turner decided against visiting it, or had he, like a modern tourist, deleted a place he had already covered? Several writers have speculated on the subject, while an old guide to Burnham of 1904 goes so far as to state that "some of that great artist's finest sky and sea paintings are taken from its beach". In the opinion of the artistically informed, Turner may have painted Burnham's and Weston's sunsets, but entitled the paintings under other names instead of by actual placenames. Constable's best-loved picture is called "The Haywain" and not after the subject which it portrays; similarly, Burnham's sunsets may be incorporated into works whose titles give no indication of the actual locality.

Whatever the truth about the painter and Burnham, one fact is certain: Turner had a specially deep love of sunsets and sunrises, anywhere from the West Country to the heart of London. He tired neither of painting them nor of watching them. His last years were lived in London, where he is said to have gone up to his rooftop daily until his final illness, to see the sun rise over London and the Thames, and again in the evening to watch the sky redden in the west. Throughout his works the sky glows with the colours of evening and morning, as much as the light of noon. Would a painter so enamoured of this aspect of nature have neglected a coastline famous for its sunset spectacles, while already painting nearby in Devon, or inland Somerset?

Burnham-Without, the adjoining parish, strangely enough does not belong to Burnham-on-Sea, being included in the vast administrative district of Axbridge. It is a very different Burnham, part of the fertile alluvial levels of mid-Somerset and therefore a dairying community. Staring at one cow across a ditch while she placidly stares back does the refugee from city life as much good as the exhilarating moorland air.

Much of the Parrett and Brue estuary country is a national nature reserve, including miles of the salt-flats where birds swoop and cry, some of them rare. The offshore Stert Island is part of the reserve.

In 1833 the short-lived Glastonbury Canal came, opened with the usual flag-waving patriotism of the 19th century, allowing export from the interior of the county of cider, corn, and cheese for the lunch packets of miners across the Channel. Already the canal age was dying and the railway age taking over. The Somerset and Dorset joint Railway from Burnham via Highbridge to Glastonbury survived until only a few decades ago; the slipway onto the beach, in direct line with the station, has railway lines embedded in its stones, marking the days when freight was loaded onto cargo boats from the local goods train.

The railway is closed now, and with it a happy chapter in many people's young lives. Seeing the familiar station in the last stages of demolition, I could have wept for the days of slow steam trains and Sunday School outings; the tiny platform remained, the rubble of the station piled over it and spilling onto the grass-grown track. Never again would the little engines from Glastonbury slide to a halt in a cloud of hot steam within sight of the sea, after the slow haul across the peaty moors through tiny wayside stations: Ashcott, Shapwick, Edington Junction. No more would the trains puff and pant, hauling a couple of carriages plus wagons into which village porters heaved heavy crates of farm produce or boxes labelled "Fragile: with care" with equal unconcern for the contents. Nor would the Sunday School specials run again, bursting with children from Street, Glastonbury, and outlying villages. Glastonbury station was unused but intact when I saw it last, looking almost as though the little train from Wells might puff in to link with the grandly named London train, actually only a connection to the main line at Templecombe. The signboard "Glastonbury and Street" was gone, but a beautiful mass of pink roses had rooted to smother the rusting supports in sweet radiance. I prefer not to visit it again; memory and the mind's eye are happier things than the rude truth of decay and dereliction.

All abandoned country railways bring on nostalgia in those who knew them, such as the quaint Cheddar Valley line from Yatton, where crates of strawberries and baskets of live poultry mingled with human passengers, waiting for the leisurely run to Wells. Only once did I hear of such a line suddenly producing an express train, in what became known as the mad engine-driver episode, though I cannot recall which of the several Somerset branch lines was the scene. The driver of a small steam locomotive, the story goes, suddenly went mad on the footplate, the fireman fighting a double fight for his life and that of the train. Flames roaring in the boiler, it careered through several stations at an unheard-of speed, lurching as the brave fireman fought for the controls. Eventually he brought the train, panting as if exhausted after its brief taste of the express life, to a shuddering halt.

Two of the three coastal B's, Berrow and Brean, really go together, a string of holiday camps, caravan sites, and chalets strung along the straight coastline. Critical conservationist eyes call this long ribbon development an eyesore along what was a lovely lonely coast, but thousands of ordinary holidaymakers derive much pleasure from this relaxing type of vacation. There is still beauty enough to justify turning a blind eye to mankind's architectural blunders; miles of firm wet sands where riders gallop their horses full tilt all the way to Burnham; the double benefit of sea air on one hand and country air on the other; lazing in sun-warmed sandy hollows; the swish of the sea if it is near, and a glittering mirror almost to the horizon if the tide is out as the sun catches the mud banks; pony rides and donkey rides; and above all, room to move and be free.

Berrow has a unique ancient church, on the dunes, the sands piled against the very walls of the churchyard. Brean, too, has an interesting coastal church, a reminder of many shipwreck tragedies of the past; part of the churchyard is given to the graves of drowned sailors. The village is a little more self-contained and compact than Berrow. Once it consisted of eight houses; now its summer population must number thousands accommodated in caravans and camps. So far and no farther does the coastal strip go; Brean Down stands firmly in the path of humanity saying "Enough!". From this point nature is the ruler, abetted by the National Trust.

Brean Down, a long promontory jutting at right-angles out of the foreshore beyond the far low water mark, has wonderful walks on springy dry turf, with birds and a wealth of wild flowers for interest. A prehistoric hill fort is only to be expected on such a vantage point; a Roman-British temple has also been discovered. Brean Down has a small place in more modern history; from here, in 1897, radio messages were transmitted across the sea to Wales, ten miles away, then the longest distance across water that a radio message had been received.

And so to the last B of the Severn Sea, Brent Knoll, a couple of miles inland from Berrow. The all-dominating landmark rises almost volcano-like from the uniform flatness all around, ruling the scene from miles inland as well as from the sea. It is naturally a superb viewpoint, giving a good impression of the vastness of the country once lying under an extension of the present sea, Brent Knoll being then an island. It briefly became an island again in the 1606 winter flood when extra strong tides burst through the dunes near Burnham, inundating three score villages as it rushed 20 miles inland; the sea had returned to its ancient bed, as much as 12 feet deep in some places. On the tide rushed, even as far as Glastonbury, where a stone on St. Benedict's church used to show the water level reached. The lesson that the sea is destructive as well as beautiful was learned the hard way. The river authorities continually watch over the drainage and defences, of which the high sloping wall at Burnham is a vital part.

Unsurprisingly, Brent Knoll is crowned by an Iron Age fort. During the years of Danish marauding, local women, children and livestock sheltered there while their menfolk tackled the intruders. Legend ascribes the Knoll's origin to the Devil, relating that it is a single shovel full of earth and rock flung down while he was digging out Cheddar Gorge.

Lympsham is not a characteristic lowland village, being shaded by a wealth of fine old trees. Before the first bridge was built the Axe was crossed by ferry; near this point stands the Hobbs Boat Inn, which according to hearsay recalls Hubba's boat, Hubba being a Danish leader when the district was plagued by their sudden and efficient raiding expeditions.

The Bristol Channel coast stretches from Brent Knoll's high viewpoint as far as the Quantocks and the Devon border, but as that part of the country lies outside the scope of this book, let us instead turn northwards to the far side of Brean Down, leaving the quiet sand dunes and open beaches of the three resorts between the Parrett and that conspicuous headland, to sample the very contrasted pleasures of eternally popular Weston-super-Mare.

Weston-super-Mare
Cinderella and Sandcastles

8

"OH, we do love to be beside the seaside": the very sound of the whistleable tune conjures up visions of a brass band oompahing on the "Prom, prom, prom, tiddley om, pom, pom"; crowds jostling onto that essentially British structure the seaside pier; candy floss; donkey rides; digging sandcastles; hats inscribed with supposedly rude captions; the seaside resort of Edwardian or between-the-wars England. If ever a town summed up that type of traditional British resort, while yet discreetly adapting itself to the wants of the current generation, it is Weston-super-Mare. The complete district was, in the latter part of the 20th century, officially allied to county of Avon, though spiritually and geographically Weston remained in popular affection still a Somerset resort. Now Avon has been disbanded and Weston resides in the region named North Somerset.

To day or weekend trippers it consists simply of the two piers, the main beaches, and the central promenade. A longer stay allows time for exploration of some local points of interest, in between the great number of available excursions farther afield and enjoying the sands, but those who have known the place over a period of years realise that there is more to Weston than meets the excursionist's eye, dating back not to the first pier and the first bathing suits, but far back into the first centuries A.D. They know, too, that Weston like most parts of Somerset has its legends, undimmed by the brilliantly illuminated and determinedly holiday-spirited Weston that is today.

Three places in one is Weston-super-Mare: the crowded trippers' stretch from the Grand Pier to the other pier, Birnbeck; south of the Grand Pier, once the deck-chaired horde has been shaken off, is Weston number two, a straight sweep of firm beaches all the way to far Uphill, a marvellously exhilarating walk by the waves in tonic air;

89

near Birnbeck Pier begins a third Weston, where the coast road plunges suddenly into thick woodlands, with the sea gleaming below through the foliage. Thus three-sided Weston can safely boast of having something for everybody, from the boisterous to the peaceable, within its borders.

In 1800 the population of what was then a fishing village barely touched the hundred mark. Within a century the inhabitants numbered about 19,000. The coming of the railway sealed its future in three respects; residential, industrial, and as a pleasure resort; modern Weston began to expand.

Set partly on the wooded slopes of Worlebury Hill, Weston-super-Mare (Wessun, in Somerset pronunciation) is a spacious town on a wide sandy bay facing into the Bristol Channel; it is said that nothing stands between it and North America. Much Regency and Victorian architecture survives, preserving the old-fashioned seaside image; modernisation contains itself proportionately within this framework. So far no skyscraper block has distorted the line of the promenade, as has happened elsewhere.

Central Weston dedicates itself entirely to the entertainment of the "beside the seaside" kind of visitor, particularly on the Grand Pier; having no water under it for part of every tide, it makes no pretence at being of maritime use, giving itself to amusements from the entrance onwards. It is lined with hot-dog, candy floss, icecream and souvenir stalls, doling out snacks and balloons to a mass of jostling humanity on summer weekends.

The far end has a complete fun-fair under cover; everything expected of a good travelling fair is ingeniously crammed into the big hall.

The adjacent promenades are equally thronged with crowds who enjoy being with more crowds, patronising the many shops and cafes between this and the Birnbeck Pier. On the sands the famous donkeys and pony carts do roaring trade from Easter onwards. Just south of the Grand Pier are a few attractive old-style snackbars on the sands, the seating being long wooden benches at timber tables. They have been there as long as most people can remember, including during the War.

What else is there to do in Weston? Apart from sunbathing in the tonic air that helped make it a health resort, as the number of convalescent homes and sanatoria confirms, there is ten-pin bowling; theatres and cinemas; and amusements of every kind. Also, it is an outstanding touring centre for the best of the West; Cheddar, Wells, Glastonbury, Wookey Hole, the lions of Longleat, and Bath are within moderate distance, while the exquisite Wye Valley is now reached across the second Severn Crossing, a marvel of modern engineering.

Steamer excursions into Devon and across to Wales were part of the Weston scene for as long as many of us can remember. For years these were operated by the delightful paddle-steamers Cardiff Queen and Bristol Queen. Unknowingly, I must have enjoyed some of the last trips on these slim, elegant Queens in 1966, for both were withdrawn soon after. Until the loss of the Queen steamers, Welsh day-excursionists awaited their return boats in the evening, singing in the bars on the pierhead as only Welshmen can. The more Somerset cider lapped inside them, the better they sang. Now with the second Severn crossing linking Bristol with South Wales, the majority of the town's many Welsh visitors come by road.

Like Burnham, Weston has sunsets of outstanding beauty when there is both sun and a certain amount of cloud. The area of Birnbeck Pier is an ideal location for this free spectacle as the low sun makes a fiery path all the way to Wales; sometimes nature seems to be deliberately playing to the gallery, as every shade from lemon to scarlet in turn touches the clouds. As the brilliant afterglow fades, the town's illuminations come on, while the offshore islands turn navy blue and fade into night. From the now uninhabited Steep Holme, Gildas is believed to have written the first true history of Great Britain, in the 7th century.

The only thing the entertainment-conscious town cannot yet control is the sea; it does not retreat anything like as far as at Burnham, but even so it goes about a mile out at low water. The Bristol Channel tides are of particular interest, the highest tidal rise in Britain; the difference at Weston may be as much as 42 feet. The exceptional tidal range on the Channel is believed to be responsible for the outstanding healthiness of the air. If high tide comes during the afternoon, the sea is a glittering, dazzling swell of diamonds, all the lovelier for having had to await its coming. First one senses a faint persistent swish far out, as the waves roll in and become bigger, breaking at last against the sea wall.

The hours of low tide are far from wasted; there are broad beaches for sandcastle digging, and the beloved Weston donkeys. From several stands on the beach the little creatures take riders from babies to teenagers, moving off in a close huddle like the start of a crowded race. Each group has its own territory, where they take their dinner of fresh hay from large wire baskets. Then it is off for more patient

Traditional horse-drawn carriages at Weston-super-Mare.

hours of trotting, guided by the stick-waving donkey boys whose occasional thwacks against furry rumps are not very convincing. Often there will be a baby donkey with its mother, as they apparently dislike being left at home while the others go to the beach. One morning I was lucky enough to meet one only 14 hours old, born the previous night; the owner was as proud as a new father, despite having been up all night supervising the delivery; a Weston donkey man truly loves his donkeys.

A chat with a local donkey man reveals a wealth of interesting facts about them and their personalities. One told me the story of the markings on their backs. Every donkey, he said, bears the cross down its back and across its shoulders, in remembrance of Palm Sunday when a humble ass carried its most distinguished Passenger into Jerusalem: "Behold, thy King cometh unto thee, meek and sitting upon an ass". When Christ dismounted, the legend says, His mount bore the sign of the cross foreshadowing the events to come. Every donkey since has had this marking; on dark fur it is barely discernible, especially under the saddlery, but on a pale coat is quite distinct. Last year I met another baby donkey on whose creamy coat was a bold brown cross down the spine and across the shoulders. Dark or light, the sign is there, I was told, though not always as distinct as on this serene young animal.

From the foregoing pages, Weston-super-Mare might appear to be noisy and extrovert, which it is in high summer along the central parades and beaches. But a completely different Weston begins only a few yards from Birnbeck Pier, where the 300 or more acres of wooded Worlebury Hill descend to the sea. Walk a little way through the toll-gate, and you are on a forest road, a road to peace, history, and legend.

Worlebury Hill is noted for its large Iron-Age fort, covering about ten acres; the pits dug for food storage and as shelter for women and children are easily identifiable. Roman relics discovered suggest that they later took it over as a lookout or fort. A number of ancient skeletons found in the camp showed wounds; they presumably died in some gruesome massacre in the very distant past.

The toll road under the hill is very beautiful; though local buses run through to Kewstoke and Sand Bay, it should if possible be walked at least one way. Only on foot can one appreciate the dense woods piled upwards to the summit, and the sea heaving on the other hand, seen through dark foliage. Weston's streets could well be on the other side of Somerset instead of only the other side of the hill.

Kewstoke is old England personified, the little church daydreaming under a protecting background of deep woods, old stone cottages huddled around it. Hens cackle and scratch; a cow moos somewhere; there is perfect peace here, where one dog taking himself for a walk may well have the lane for his own. The Monks' Steps, sometimes called St. Kew's Steps, are an ancient rise of about 200 rocky steps, a hard slog to a superb view. They supposedly lead to where St. Kew had a little hermitage on an eyrie with half northern Somerset below him and only Heaven above. Other authorities say they are of pre-Roman date, while the most commonly held theory is that they led to the remote Woodspring Priory, beyond Sand Bay.

Kewstoke held a sacred link with the priory, unknowingly, for several centuries, hidden there at the Dissolution as the Priory's most precious possession. The treasure, the Becket Cup or Kewstoke Reliquary, is of no distinguished design, nor chased with gold; it is not even complete, being just an old broken wooden vessel. The contents make it priceless; human bloodstains, believed to be the life-blood of the murdered Archbishop, brought from Canterbury. Woodspring Priory was one of a series of expiatory foundations built during the long repentance for a hasty sin by a grandson of one of St. Thomas Becket's original four murderers. Experts agree that the stains may be what was called Canterbury Water, in which the blood of the martyr was mixed. The relic is in Taunton Museum now.

The wooden cup was brought to Kewstoke church from the Priory as the destruction of the Dissolution loomed nearer, where some unknown person secreted it behind a small carving, so well that it lay there unsuspected for several centuries.

Woodspring Priory itself is remote even today, far out on the flat grasslands inland from Sand Bay, cradled in pastures and acres of growing crops. Following the Reformation it became a house and farm, incorporating the battlemented walls, the tithe barn, and the unusual square tower. Wick St. Lawrence is equally remote and unspoiled; here we come back to the Somerset moors again, to the country of dykes and pastures. The village is noted for its cider-apple orchards, but, ironically, has no public house. Like much of low-lying Somerset, this area was once either under water or mire; a local story tells of a horse and rider caught in the tidal bog, sinking deeper as the tide rose, surrounded them, and with agonising slowness drowned them. Such tales are often told of the tidal flats; I remember seeing a lovely Reynolds-like portrait of three young sisters in a Somerset mansion. "What lovely children!" my companion exclaimed. Soon after its completion, the owner related, one child became caught in coastal mire; her two sisters in trying to save her were also trapped, and all three were drowned.

An increasing number of people come to the quiet country north of Weston, especially to Sand Bay. As at Weston the tide goes well out, leaving a mile-wide expanse of pale sand, hence its name, but at high tide Sand Bay is glorious: the breakers roll straight in from the Atlantic, the sun shining through them like a million diamonds, the long wooded Worlebury Hill closing one side of the bay with a green and beautiful background.

The thin line of coastal houses offends the eyes of those who would prefer so lovely a bay unspoiled; on the other hand, they give great pleasure for holidays or retirement to many people who want a seaside residence in peace and tonic air yet near enough to a town to enjoy its facilities at will.

After Kewstoke the lovely road from Weston Woods emerges into the countryside behind Sand Bay; the steep hanging woods merge into pastoral slopes and then into flat moors, beyond which Clevedon stands on its headland beyond another fine bay. Unlike the central moors, these have hedges as well as dykes to form a criss-cross pattern. It all seems far from civilised Weston here, a stretch smelling softly of grass, hay and a suspicion of pig, where one bark or a sudden cackle of hens sounds on the peaceful air. In reality Weston's outskirts lurk just ahead, round the landward curve of Worlebury Hill.

Weston number three starts south of Grand Pier; the crowds thin out, and there are about two miles of firm sands inviting the visitor to take a seaboard walk to historic Uphill. Uphill's cliff-top church is a local landmark, many walkers' goal for its roofless but interesting self and for the fine views from the churchyard over the sea to Wales. Legend here takes over from the amusement arcades of central Weston, as it did at Kewstoke, based on the Devil as a change from saints. To discourage Christianity, the Devil constantly removed the stones of a church being built beneath the cliff to the top of the hill, hoping to extinguish the faith through aching human muscles, giving the place its name, Up-Hill. Our ancestors being of stern stuff accepted the new site. In the present century, when the explosion of urbanisation sent Weston sprawling out to Uphill, another attempt was made to construct a church on the level: so far the Devil has not laid hands on it.

Uphill cliff, the last outpost of the Mendips, guards the mouth of the little River Axe, where was a Roman port. It is assumed that this was where Joseph of Arimathea would normally have put in before turning inland towards the Somerset lagoons, the Mendip lead mines, or Avalon. If the belief that he brought the Boy Christ on some of his business voyages to England is true, then "the Countenance Divine" that shone forth "upon those clouded hills" must have fallen first on Uphill.

The history and geography of ancient Somerset show that during the so-called lost years of His life, He could have sailed at some time on His uncle's boat, when he called at the port on the Axe before going on to his lead mine on Mendip. The ancient road from Old Sarum across the lead-yielding Mendips in fact terminated at this harbour, where cargo was loaded for shipment to the East. I once sailed up the Bristol Channel on a steamer in company with a young clergyman, as deeply interested in the Arimathea stories as I; from far out, the low coast was below the horizon, only Steep Holme and Brent Knoll being in view in the distance, the latter also appearing to be an island. Did we see what Jesus saw, sailing up towards the Axe? It was a deep thought to ponder, which my companion had already determined to incorporate into his next sermon.

Uphill was inhabited earlier still, by beasts unknown in historic times. It was famous for a bone-filled cave, tragically destroyed by quarrying, which yielded remains of rhino, bear, bison, and the wild boar. Quarrying destroyed a similar rock fissure at nearby Bleadon, where bones discovered included those of wolves, tigers, and a giant cave-bear; the latter, the bones show, stood nearly three metres tall.

Uphill is not all legend; it is a marvellous sailing centre too. Here can be seen the rather un-British sport of sand-yachting on the wide firm breezy beaches. It is exciting to watch, a sport demanding considerable skill and judgment, so fast do the yachts flash across the beach, white sails flying like gulls on the wing.

Candy floss, slot machines, and jostling crowds are the extrovert filling in the sandwich that is Weston-super-Mare, the outer layers being quiet Kewstoke and Sand Bay, and historic Uphill. As with other sandwiches, if you do not like the filling, try another flavour; perhaps a farm holiday a little way inland, or caravanning at Brean, on the other side of Brean Down.

It can fairly safely be said that almost anyone can discover something to like in or near Weston, whether it be building sandcastles and riding in Cinderella's coach, discovering byways of history, or mingling with the "let's be matey" types on the piers. And that is as good a boast as any seaside resort could hope to make.

Downside and Shepton Mallet
Benedicts and Babycham

"I'll never forget!" In practice, the event we are convinced will be unforgettable often slips into limbo before its first anniversary comes round. Most of us have only a handful of memories which, tried against time, prove genuinely evergreen. I can number my own on less than five fingers: the first sight of the snowy Jungfrau piercing celestially blue skies like an incandescently shining mass of white icecream; standing humbled in the tiny attic where Beethoven was born; being caught 7,000 feet up on the Alps while a thunderstorm raged above and below at the same time; and being almost alone in Downside Abbey as the monks' midday worship brushed nearly four centuries aside as if they had never been.

While holidaying in mid-Somerset I and a companion were determined to see this wonderful modern monastery, where the Benedictine Rule that was broken off with the destruction of Glastonbury at the Reformation had in a sense picked up the threads of the past, within a few miles of the ruined Abbey.

The journey was not excessive as the crow flies, but we being neither crows nor motorists it posed its problems, one link in a chain of buses running only at three-hourly intervals. Eventually we arrived at Stratton-on-the-Fosse, straddling the historic Fosse Way but otherwise an undistinguished village overshadowed by Downside Abbey.

Stone towers rose from meadows of lushest green, thick with buttercups, seen through arches of lazily stirring branches. The drowsy noon silence gave a very real impression of the atmosphere the villagers living in the shadow of some great monastery must have known in the Middle Ages, a deeper peace than mere absence of noise.

The Abbey Church at Downside.

At the very door of the Abbey church, disappointment struck, in the shape of a small announcement that it was closed to visitors at this hour. Closed, and the only practicable return bus left before it reopened: our carefully dovetailed cross-country trip was wasted. Then a young priest appeared; he thought for a moment, smilingly produced a massive key, and let us in, relocking the door. Thanks to him we saw the Abbey after all, and thanks to him our journey ended by stepping back into history, like taking two tickets into the past.

Downside empty breathed sanctity; not piously dutiful, but the real thing, giving stone walls that elusive quality which is immediately felt – or found to be absent – on entering a great church or cathedral. Some glorious historic buildings may be superb architectural studies, marvels of craftsmanship without souls; over others, though ruined for centuries, and trodden by tourists instead of monks, atmosphere clings like a physical thing, as at Glastonbury. A few – a very few – modern churches have that quality, such as Downside.

Quietly we explored the high, narrow, shadowy nave, admiring the beauty of simplicity and restraint, and some of the chapels adorned with a fortune in silver, alabaster, and embroidery. We came to the beautiful Lady Chapel, approached by wide steps and wondrously wrought-iron gates, and there the silence was broken. Somewhere the monks were chanting. The voices came nearer, with the swish of sandalled feet on stone floors, the unseen singers approaching from the Abbey buildings. Time did not stand still then: it swept us back into the 15th century in a moment. Hastily we slipped into a dim corner of the empty nave as the robed brothers entered chanting, processing into the choir to observe their noon office, watched only by two women, perhaps intruders. We were uncertain on this point, hence the hasty retreat into the shades. The monks took their dignified places, their voices rising, falling, and dissolving into the high vaulting. The famous organ might have dispelled the illusion of time frozen, but on that day the music was unaccompanied, the prayers subdued, the "Amens" hushed. It was as though they and we were petrified into an ageless tableau that was neither past, present nor future, but eternity.

Their devotions over, the monks departed with unhurried orderliness. We, too, had to leave, pausing only to gaze again at the grey pile towering over immaculate lawns and grassy banks, before turning for the bus-stop. We did not say much then: there is little to say but a lot to think on when returning from living history to the current day.

Any guide-book to Somerset will give the usual architectural description and facts about Downside, but no guide can find its soul as can a silent personal visit in a dreamy noon.

There is a lovely touch of coincidence about Downside's being so near Glastonbury. The desolation and ruin following the Dissolution seemed to be the end of the monastic life for the vast Abbey, its spreading estates, and its priceless library and treasures; never again would Benedictine monks live in brotherhood in Somerset. Fate, though, plays strange games with people and places; in 1814 a community of Benedictine monks, driven back to England in the turmoil of the French Revolution from Douai, settled at Stratton and began building the nucleus from which sprang the present modern but traditionally-built church. The Dissolution was not an end, but an interruption, the Benedictine Rule being picked up again in the 19th and 20th centuries almost within sight of ruined Glastonbury. Abbot Whiting is remembered in the wonderful church that has revived his Order so near his own Abbey; Downside's beautiful chapel of the English Martyrs is often spoken of as the chapel of Blessed Richard Whiting. He, having been beatified by the Catholic Church, is entitled to be called Blessed; the canonisation of certain English martyrs by the reigning Pope raises the hopes of many people that Whiting may some day be elevated to the title of Saint. The church, bigger than some cathedrals, was completed in 1935 apart from minor later additions, in a simple style emphasising height through the narrowness of the nave and the large number of pointed arches.

The attached Downside School is one of the best known Catholic schools in England. Here again is a parallel with Glastonbury and other Medieval foundations, when the monasteries were the only true seats of learning, possessing wonderful libraries, with literate monks to teach the young and to practice the art of illumination of manuscripts. Downside, combining church, community and education within one group of buildings thus follows a Medieval pattern even in this information age.

Glastonbury Abbey, Wells Cathedral, Axbridge's fine old church, and several other Somerset masterpieces of church building, are of Doulting stone, the creamy-grey product of the Doulting quarries near Shepton Mallet. The quarries were given by King Ine of Wessex to Glastonbury Abbey far back in the 8th century, in memory of the king's nephew St. Aldhelm, who died at Doulting. St. Aldhelm's dying words to the monks who surrounded him were the wish to be taken into the little wooden church, and there he breathed his last. It was later rebuilt in stone, and again by the Normans. The quarries continued in Glastonbury's estates for many centuries; stone from Doulting was being used for yet more work on the already magnificent Abbey on the very eve of its downfall.

Today Somerset stone is still in demand. Chunks of the Mendips are seen from the Chelsea Flower Show, in the form of garden urns and ballusters, to Turkey where the surfaces of the mighty Bosphorus Bridge are dressed with Mendip basalt chippings. 3,000 tons of exported Somerset went into that huge span linking Turkey with Greece, this type of chipping being considered so superior for anti-skid surfaces that shipping many loads all the way from Sharpness Docks to the gateway of Asia was a worthwhile venture.

From the worlds of stone quarrying, church building and Benedictine monks we can come back to the present with a bump by taking the road to nearby Shepton Mallet, an old town at heart that keeps apace of contemporary industry and commerce, including manufacture of a drink which came into its own in the 1970s and 80s, but which is still internationally popular today. The story of Babycham's creation by four Shepton Mallet brothers is a classic obscurity-to-riches fairytale. Appropriately, the product's trademark is also something from fairyland, a tiny prancing little deer that looks like something from a story book but has no exact counterpart in the real animal world.

The Showerings were an old Shepton Mallet family, brewers, cider makers and innkeepers almost two centuries before Babycham was born. Four brothers – Arthur, Herbert, Francis and Ralph – entered into the still-modest family business just before the war, and began thinking on broader lines for the future, experimenting with various soft drinks. It was not until the 1950s that they evolved the perry that was to make the firm world famous and the brothers wealthy industrial kings. They were their own publicity men and market researchers, quietly watching its sales over bars in the Bristol area. An important discovery was that the new drink was welcomed by women and young people, who had formerly felt out of place at a public bar, the drink having the sparkle of a light wine yet being non-alcoholic.

To prove its worth, the Showerings entered their new perry in every major agricultural show in the country, and every time it took first prize. It also took the championship of the Royal Agricultural Society: it was a young champion, a baby champ. Thus the name Babycham arrived on the scene.

Babycham is based on pear juices, but with the sparkle of champagne. In the 1970s it gave Shepton Mallet an industrial uplift, the factory having all the latest equipment, a cross between a ship's engine room, an ultra-sterile laboratory, and an airport control room.

Shepton Mallet is not only Babycham. One of the first postwar offshoots of Clarks' shoe factory was opened there; the site, taken over after Army use, included eight old Army huts, converted to temporary industrial use. Only a week later the first production started; by 1954 about 1,900,000 pairs of shoes were being made annually, and figures have constantly risen since. The town has progressed a lot since its old bacon-producing days, and since it saw something of the ugliness of the Industrial Revolution and its Spinning-Jenny riots.

Once it was a wool town, as the prosperous merchants' houses and church indicate. So does its name, formerly Sheep-town. There is a fine 16th-century market cross, though wives are no longer sold in the square like cattle. Today it is a three-faced town; ancient and grey walled round the centre, industrial on the outskirts, and agricultural beyond the last houses. Agriculture means not only growing crops and rearing cattle, but something on a huge scale, Shepton Mallet being now the permanent home of the Bath and West Show.

The Bath and West site is vast, as any aerial photograph shows, and in general the tendency is towards more entries and more visitors each year. There are classes for sheep, goats, poultry and pigeons, and for farm products like cheese and honey, as well as demonstrations of sheep-shearing, forestry, and horse-shoeing. There are many attractions for the general public as well as countrymen, including show jumping, parachuting and special events. One Show included a spectacular jousting tournament by mounted and armoured knights, and a sentimental look back to Victorian days with steam engines and fairground rides – some manned by people in Victorian costume – and a World of Nature exhibition dating from the Great Exhibition of 1851, originally shown at the Crystal Palace.

Shepton Mallet is cradled in the rolling foothills of the eastern Mendips, a gentle mild country of fine rich pastures and old stone villages. One of the best known is Croscombe, for the lavish Jacobean carving in its church. All is elaborately decorated: pulpit, box-pews, screen and roof. Much of it is coloured, as was discovered when the wonders of modern art restoration revealed almost hidden beauty beneath layers of centuries-old grime and weathering. Croscombe (the name probably incorporates the Welsh "cwm" meaning a coombe or valley) was a cloth weaving centre in the past, hence a larger and more lavishly furnished church than is expected of a village. Like many others in the area, it is partly of Doulting stone.

On the road to Wells is also Dinder, pastoral old England dreaming among rich fields and running streams. It is all mellow stone cottages, with a manor house and ancient church, every American's idea of rural England, though few of them see it once they have said a breathless Hello and Goodbye to Wells en route to the next stop. It is worth spending a morning pottering around little Dinder; how then can one see Wells in an even shorter time, when it has enough secrets to last the explorer a month, and a cathedral that shows new facets to those who have known it for years?

10

Wells

Singing Boys and Ringing Swans

A precious jewel in a worthy setting, like a priceless heirloom brooch; so a Somerset man once summed up Wells. It is as good a description as any, the peerless Cathedral being the centrepiece with a circle of lesser but still valuable pieces grouped about it – the gateways, the moated Palace, the closes and the gracious town; the whole being mounted on a setting of emeralds – the lawns before the West Front, the parklands and meadows, the Mendips protecting it to the north and the open breezy moors to the south.

Precious; priceless; peerless: a fair slice of the thesaurus must have been used by countless writers trying to describe the indescribable, because words can only paint a physical picture; it is less easy to capture atmosphere and spirit in words when writing of a town like Wells that has so much besides the Cathedral and so many faces besides that of the Church. Personally I have known it since the age of seven, and still find something fresh on every return visit.

If Wells is like a jewelled brooch, then it is natural to look first at the principal gem, the Cathedral that is not one of our biggest but is accepted to be among the loveliest. Every souvenir shop in the town sells informative books following its history in detail; suffice it here to keep technical details to a minimum, and try to capture something of its feeling, and think of some of the people who are part of its story.

There are several possible approaches; the best is not from the Market Square but through the Ancient Gatehouse. Once under the arch, the visitor comes immediately upon the full view of the majestic West Front, set back and displayed across a wide open Green. It is one of the few major cathedrals not hemmed in by streets and shops, but shown off at a distance that reveals the full dignity and beauty of its frontage.

The famous West Front is a miracle of craftsmanship in any light, but perhaps the best of all is the pink-gold of a late spring evening when the dying sun tinges the statuary and throws the detail into black relief. If there are fast-moving clouds floating across the sky, looking up gives the strange impression that it is the Cathedral that is gently sailing and moving, and not the clouds. From the Green the unique gallery of ancient sculptures can be seen entire. There are about 300 statues of princes and priests, bishops and saints; over the central door are the Virgin and Child, and above them the Coronation of the Virgin. Then come nine orders of angels, the twelve Apostles, and on the highest point the remains of a representation of Christ in majesty. Some are damaged, others in various states of preservation.

Readers familiar with Europe as well as England may have noticed an interesting parallel with the Church of the Holy Family in Barcelona, where the architect Gaudi based his fantastic turrets on the strange rock formations of Montserrat; in Cheddar Gorge is a pair of squared-off rock pinnacles linked by a straight ledge a little lower, bearing a remarkable resemblance to the unusual squared western towers of Wells and the lower tiers of sculptures between them. Coincidence? A builder's subconscious? It is an interesting point to look for when visiting the two places.

A church has stood here for 1,200 years, since King Ine, a Somerset-born king, founded a church near the springs giving Wells its name. The building we see now was begun in the 12th century. Dedicated to St. Andrew, whose blue and white flag flies often over Wells, it covers several architectural styles. Entering from the elaboration of the West Front, two things strike the eye: the gentle simplicity of the nave, and the completely unique inverted arches. All is pale light stone and many-arched elegance, the understatement of the vaulting relieved by graceful painted designs in dull red. The inverted arches dominate the nave, disliked by those who would prefer an uninterrupted full-length view, but felt by many to be the most distinctive feature of all. They were not intended so boldly to assert themselves, being simply a brilliant solution to a difficult engineering problem when in 1338 the heavy central tower, added onto foundations never intended to support such a weight, began to settle and drag the nave walls out of true with it. A normal pointed arch rises from the floor while its counterpart hangs from the roof, the two apexes meeting to form, appropriately, the St. Andrew's cross. Two large circular openings on either side of the central meeting point relieve the heaviness to the eye, and add to the interest of the geometric design.

Two exquisite chantries stand in the nave, perfect miniature churches full of delicate carving, fan-vaulting, and lace cut from cream stone. The choir translates us into yet another architectural period, the florid Decorated style. Here elaboration replaces the nave's restraint, repeated in the stained glass and in the painted organ pipework.

Wells Cathedral has a wealth of smaller points of interest, after one has duly marvelled at its overall beauty. There is miniature story-telling in stone: a man with toothache and scrumpers being caught stealing apples. The series of bishops' tombs includes that of Bishop Still who wrote "Little Jack Horner". The rhyme refers to Jack Horner, steward of the last Abbot of Glastonbury who, as well as concealing the monastery's priceless treasure at the approach of disaster, also attempted to smuggle the valuable deeds of some of the abbey's many manors to London as gifts to the king, a desperate last bid to win royal favour and reprieve glorious Glastonbury. Knowing that hostile forces were already close, the abbot reputedly concealed the deeds in a large pie, carried by the supposedly trustworthy Horner. On the way to London, temptation overcame the steward, Horner abstracted from the pie a plum for himself, the deeds to the ancient manor of Mells:

> He put in his thumb,
> And pulled out a plum,
> And said, what a clever boy am I.

Whatever the truth of the tale, it is certain that generations of Horners held Mells, and that their descendants resided there long after.

This most lovely of churches is not merely a sightseers' goal, but a place of worship; to rush through its standard features without hearing Evensong is to look at it without hearing it speak. The voices scarcely sound human, celestially caught by the vaulting, but their owners do have a normal schoolboy exterior, being not entirely averse to a scrap on the Green afterwards.

Wells is famous for its remarkable clock, whose interest is as undying to the resident as the casual visitor, never failing to fascinate. Made by some genius of the 14th century, it is a mechanical marvel that draws crowds to the north transept every quarter hour. The main face shows the 24 hours, marked by a moving gold sun; the minutes, ticked off by a faster moving star; the days of the month; and the

Wells - the Chain Gate and Cathedral.

phases of the moon. The performance starts with Jack Blandiver, a grotesque figure sitting high above, kicking small bells with his heels before striking the hour with his mallet on the bell before him. Then, on a miniature stage above the clock, armoured knights on horseback ride to clockwork battle, clickety-click as they revolve. There is another face outside the Cathedral near the Chain Gate, where two knights in armour strike the hours with battleaxes. The internal mechanism has been renewed, but being of such outstanding interest it was taken to the Science Museum in London.

Ancient and modern go in harmony in this most visited corner of the Cathedral; the crucified Christ, an interpretation of 1956, hangs immediately beneath the ancient clock. It is an immensely compelling figure, contemporary yet blending happily with the Medieval craftsmanship around it, of great dignity and symmetry.

Few cathedrals are of so many parts as Wells; the Chapter House alone is an architectural masterpiece, and the steps to it world renowned. It is like standing at the foot of a cascade of stone, pouring downwards from the bridge leading to the Close. The treads are worn by the feet of untold thousands. Cluster on cluster of slim columns support intricate arches, making the entire staircase a thing of geometrical perfection. Halfway up the flight branches, where an ingenious fan of steps leads to the Chapter House, a marvel of airy lightness. One thick pillar, its gracefully grouped columns belying its strength, supports the many ribs of the intricate vaulting, like the stem and petals of a huge stone chrysanthemum. The chamber, no lifeless study in building without a purpose, is frequently used for exhibitions promoting Christian causes and work; likewise the Cathedral itself is not coldly lifeless or its authorities opposed to its use for events stressing the beautiful things of the world for which we go there to give thanks: orchestral and choral concerts are given in the nave, by local and national ensembles, as well as occasional organ recitals.

There is still more to see within the precincts, including the finely proportioned cloisters that enclose the Palm Churchyard. The name derives from the yews growing there, sprigs of which were once used during the Palm Sunday ceremonial before dried and specially grown palms began to be imported, as they are now, from southern Europe or North Africa. The cloister walls are lined with a collection to delight epitaph collectors, many of them removed from the choir in the 19th century. One of the best known is to Thomas Linley, his daughters, and "his granddaughter Elizabeth Ann, wife of R. B. Sheridan, Esq.". It has not only literary interest; from this marriage Lord Snowdon claims a remote connection with the family, hence his and the late Princess Margaret's son's title of Viscount Linley. There are the usual tear-jerkers, such as: "The widowed consort and the orphan boy, Bereft of those pure founts of earthly joy, She a fond husband, he a father's love", or "A virtuous spouse and faithful friend, She continued to her end".

Peace is the word that comes to mind again and again when thinking of Wells; its history too has been generally uneventful, but its quiet has been disturbed a few times when conflict raged not in it but near it. During the Civil War a "multitude" entered brandishing dung-picks, pitchforks and knobbed staves, smashing the stained glass and destroying irreplaceable pictures; one painting was carried away as a trophy on the point of a spear. Monmouth's rebels briefly held the town, stabling their horses in the Cathedral nave; the desecration of the High Altar was warded off by Lord Grey who boldly defended it with drawn sword. During the Second World War a German aircraft was brought down in the fields near the Cathedral; I was told that his mission was to aim at that glorious pile. Those who saw him driven safely from his target felt a justifiable bitterness until they dragged from the wreckage a broken pathetic boy, dying to obey a command. The people of Wells, while unspeakably thankful that the Cathedral was spared, saw the pity and fruitlessness of war instead of anger: he was some mother's son. The ugliest episode in Wells' past, except perhaps for the travesty of a trial of Abbot Whiting of Glastonbury, was judge Jeffreys' Bloody Assize at the Guildhall following the Monmouth Rebellion. Scores of prisoners were herded into the Cathedral cloisters or St. Cuthbert's church before being rushed through hurried trials like human beings on a conveyor belt to misery, receiving the vicious sentences that earned the Assize its name.

Gatehouses are a special feature of Wells, dividing the Cathedral and precincts from the charming city. Two stand in the square; the Bishop's Eye leading to the moat and Palace, and Penniless Porch leading to the Green, so named from the beggars who sat there soliciting alms from passing churchgoers. Between Penniless Porch and the Ancient Gatehouse in Sadler Street is a massive wall, broken by the modern gap affording one of the best photographic angles on the West Front; it is not easily visible, houses being built back-to-back on both sides of the wall, facing outwards from it. The famous Chain Gate spans the former Bath road from the Vicars' Close, allowing the vicars to cross direct to the Chapter House. The road is now closed to through traffic, restoring the entire Cathedral area to its rightful quietness.

The Vicars' Close is reputedly unequalled in Europe, an entire street of 14th century houses in two rows of 21, each with a minute garden, entered through yet another ancient stone gatehouse. From the far end is a splendid view for photographers doing what residents call the Tourist Trot: the Cathedral towers and pinnacles with the ornate Chapter House rearing above the two rows of uniformly tall chimneys of this unique street. Also facing the Green are the castle-like Old Deanery; an interesting museum showing finds from the Mendip caves as well as local history; and the well-known Theological College opened in 1840. In 1940 the Archbishop of Canterbury attended its centenary celebrations. The College closed in 1971, to the sadness of thousands of priests who began their careers by studying there under the shadow of one of Britain's most exquisite cathedrals.

Alone in England Wells stands in having a moated and fortified Bishop's Palace, complete with drawbridge. Entering from the Square by the Bishop's Eye one meets a scene of utter tranquillity: shady trees, cropped lawns, peaceful waters from which rises a long line of turreted and battlemented walls with arrow slits, and a heavy gatehouse whose drawbridge spans the moat on massive chains. Is

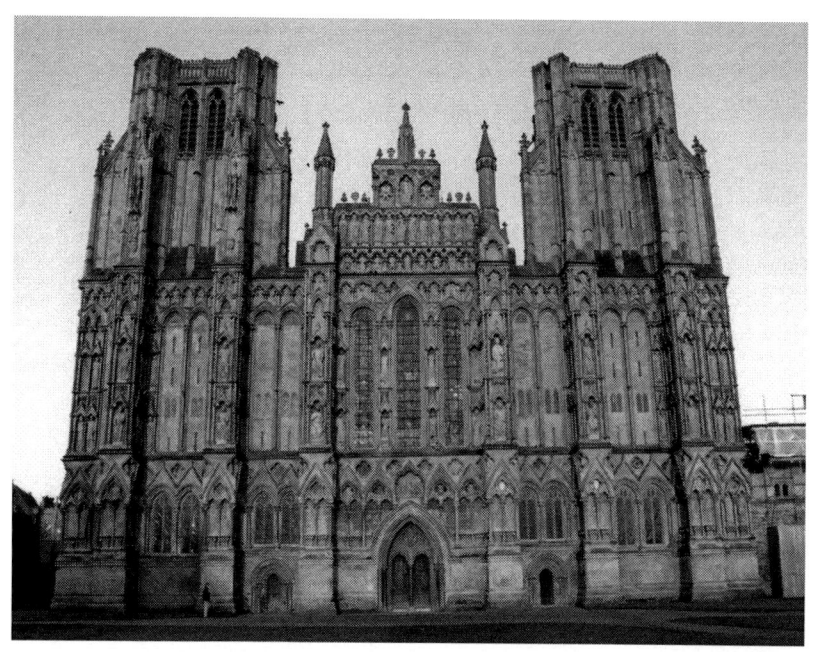

The West Front of Wells Cathedral.

this an ogre's castle or a bishop's home? Ancient trees line the banks; their roots may be dry enough to sit on in pouring rain, even if it has rained for hours so thick is the foliage. Pale green fronds sway under the water like a submerged forest of miniature trees.

Walking round the moat is the accepted evening stroll, a pleasure denied the thousands of day tourists. They have missed the most perfect end to a day in Wells – only one of many reasons why it should be given at least a weekend to reveal itself – when sharp quacks break evening silence as one walks alongside still waters to continue straight out into the countryside. One evening I arrived late from London while there was yet time for a turn round the moat at dusk; the quiet was complete, but for a nightingale singing on a stone wall. Carefully I sat down while the bird sang a series of coloratura arias over my head, pouring out endless cadenzas for an audience of one with a wall for a stage and a setting of towers and battlements such as no opera house could give such a human singer, if she existed.

If the nightingale at dusk was opera, the ruined Palace banqueting hall was ballet, the ideal setting for "Giselle". Was that a white ghost moving among the long ruined arches outlined against a darkening sky? In daylight the sight is equally romantic, for the banqueting hall was one of the noblest in England before its destruction at the Reformation. It is a lovely sight among the splendid trees and immaculate lawns, together with the private chapel and ancient Palace. This is one of Britain's oldest inhabited houses, ranging from the 13th century onwards. The fortifications were added by a 14th century bishop who was not particularly popular locally; the defences were not put to the test in actual battle, but the bridge was drawn only about 170 years ago after Reform-Act rioters destroyed the palace at Bristol.

The oldest part of the Palace was built by Bishop Jocelin who was a witness of Magna Carta. The finely proportioned Long Gallery is lined with portraits of past bishops, whom all but connoisseurs of either bishops or portraiture tend to pass over. Some of them repay a closer look, for the stories behind them. Bishop Hooper was attendant upon the Duke of Monmouth at his execution; Bishop Peter Mews was nicknamed the Fighting Bishop for his active part as an artilleryman at the Battle of Sedgemoor, and also served in Charles I's army; Bishop Still managed to become a rich man through the Mendip lead mines, eschewing priestly poverty and humility; Bishop Creighton, distantly related to Charles II, was the King's chaplain in exile; he became Dean after the previous Dean was murdered during the Civil War by a shoemaker Parliamentarian.

Bishop Ken reputedly wrote "Awake my soul and with the sun" and "Glory my God to Thee this night" in a summerhouse in the grounds. He entertained the poor at dinner every Sunday in the ruined banqueting hall. Ken was appointed by Charles II, strangely enough because the King remembered him for refusing a royal request to give hospitality to Nell Gwyn at Winchester. When the Wells seat fell vacant Charles asked: "Where is the good little man who refused lodging to poor Nell?" and promptly made him Bishop of Wells.

Bishop Ken was one of the group known to history as The Seven Bishops, who protested against James II's Declaration of Indulgence, holding it to be illegal. Ken with the other six was tried but, despite great efforts to have them found guilty, all seven were finally acquitted. This prelate is constantly remembered by congregations both Anglican and Non-conformist, not only for his two famous hymns but also for the single four-line verse known as the Doxology: "Praise God from whom all blessings flow".

The Coronation Cope is on show in the Palace, worn for the Coronations of Edward VII, George V, George VI and our present

Queen. The Bishop of 1953 being a tall man, the cope was cleverly lengthened, the join only being noticeable if pointed out. Close inspection shows how ingeniously the embroidery was carried into the false hem; even the embroiderers' original design markings can be seen. At Richard I's Coronation, Bishop Reginald of Wells, as one of the senior bishops, took a suitably prominent position at the ceremony. Ever since, the Bishop of Bath and Wells has stood at the Monarch's left hand at successive Coronations.

The Drawing Room, used for meetings, has a superb carpet of pink, elaborately patterned; it was designed for another palace, the glittering Crystal Palace, when it was opened for the Great Exhibition of 1851. The Crystal Palace, rebuilt in southeast London, died as spectacularly as it had lived in a terrible inferno close to my present home; it was strange to find this link between two homes, one in Somerset and one in Kent, on a floor in Wells, and looking in astonishingly good condition for its age. A fragment of Wells was incorporated into one of the finest features of the great Crystal Palace building, the series of courts devised in the manners of various nations and architectural periods: Roman, Greek, Assyrian, Byzantine, German, Pompeiian. Among the best was the English Medieval Court designed by Wyatt, entered through a reproduction of the west door of Tintern Abbey which lead into the cloister of Guisborough Abbey. Unlike the countless statues adorning the Palace and grounds, the figures here were copies of genuine Medieval work, taken from two of the leading churches of that time; to the left, figures copied from Westminster Abbey, and to the right statues from the West Front of Wells. Thus generations of Londoners and their children became familiar with a little of the grandeur that is Wells as they strolled amid the grandeur that was the Crystal Palace.

The Wells Palace possesses the chair supposedly used by Abbot Whiting at his travesty trial, whose outcome had already been fixed, in the great banqueting hall, the most shameful event ever to desecrate this peaceful city. Brought back from the Tower of London to be tried for supposedly withholding the Glastonbury treasures, Abbot Whiting's fate was decided by Cromwell in advance: "The Abbot of Glaston to be tried … and also executed there". The charge against the frail old man was treason.

That day in 1539 the hall was in its full splendour, having been used for many a ceremonious entertaining of high Church dignitaries but never for such a mockery of justice. The trial dragged on all day, duly debating the charges of "fraudulent conveyance of the Abbey goods" and of treason. The pre-arranged death sentence was passed on the aged Abbot and two fellow monks, the means to be hanging, drawing and quartering on Glastonbury Tor. Looking at the graceful arches and long windows now surrounded by rustling trees, the interior carpeted with velvet grass, the roof open to the sky, it is difficult to realise that so dark a shadow once disgraced so matchless a place.

Today all around the Palace is green peace. The grounds have the springs from which Wells takes its name, eternally bubbling up from the soft sand under a glass-clear pool before tumbling over a weir to form the moat; it is in this pool that the Cathedral is reflected in the best-known of all picture-postcard views, that taken from the southeast.

Many come to Wells from across the Atlantic, fall in love with it, and want to leave something of themselves there; others, stationed in the vicinity in the war, return to it in peacetime and delight to find it unchanged. Facing the moat are a number of public seats presented by Americans, bearing small plaques naming their donors; one is from a couple in Florida, one from Pasadena, another from Riverside, California, and a fourth from a resident of Los Angeles; so does the town insinuate itself into the affections of those who have known it. One American called it "the one place in England that is perfect", and spent the rest of his holiday investigating every house for sale he came across.

Watching the clocks work is a perennial pleasure for all who come to what Elizabeth Goudge called "A City of Bells"; one of the other chief attractions is bell ringing of a different nature, when the swans ring for their food with their own beaks at the Palace gatehouse. A real Swan Lake ballet is danced by birds wearing natural tutus of snowy feathers, congregating at feeding times under a narrow window where dangles an inviting bell-pull. Suddenly a sinuous neck stretches up, and a determined beak grasps the handle; the swan's businesslike tug sets off a tinkling chime. Beady eyes watch expectantly as the casement opens and food is thrown to the ringer and her corps-de-ballet. It has been said that the daughter of a Victorian Bishop taught them the trick, but ancient glass at Nailsea implies that this bell ceremony has been performed for about five centuries: maybe the Bishop's daughter revived a custom that had for some reason lapsed. The bell-ringing swans delight today's children as their grandparent swans amused our own grandparents. We who fortunately knew Wells at that most impressionable age of youth retain a lasting love for it, not least for memories of a moated Palace where swans ring for their supper.

Too many of our cathedral cities are hemmed in by streets and traffic, not allowing the central interest to stand back and be admired as at Wells, where the Cathedral is separated from the town by its many ancient gates. Immediately outside the walls is a market square faced by gracious old houses, antique shops, and ancient inns, including the exceptionally picturesque Crown, too often overlooked in a brief tour. The main street is winding and cheery, with numerous former coaching inns that are now delightful places for a drink and a rest. Above the broad square, where a small market is notable for its china stalls, the Cathedral towers soar majestically, making this one of the West Country's most photographed scenes. The most unusual feature is the conduit, where water from the wells in the Palace grounds eternally trickles down before running along the gutters on either side of the main street, keeping it always fresh and clean; first-time tourists, gazing ahead at the beautiful combination of old houses, medieval gates and pinnacled towers often miss this minor feature under foot.

Many feet tread on a further piece of history, their owners being naturally more intent on the scene before them, a piece of history dating only from 1964. In that year a Wells girl, already an athletics star at home, journeyed to far away Tokyo, there to set up a world record. Mary Bignal-Rand, since known as the Golden Girl of Wells, has her achievement recorded in the pavement outside the row of shops near Penniless Porch. A long golden frieze, the length of a dozen paving stones, makes a pattern of Olympic rings interspersed with the English rose and the St. Andrew's cross of Wells. A plaque records that this "represents the world-record ladies' long jump made by Mary Bignal-Rand, a native of this city, to win the gold medal at the Olympic Games, Tokyo 1964. It is 22 feet 21 inches long, and is placed here in admiration of her achievement". Seeing the actual distance jumped gives a true idea of the size of her winning leap. Surprising Somerset again: where else can one expect to walk on the history of the 20th century while gazing at the creation of hundreds of years of human craftsmanship at the same time?

The whole town is full of byways and ancient inns, in themselves worth exploring. In the evenings, when traffic has died down to a murmur, it is pleasant to stroll at random down a side turning, probably to find something new and interesting. All is quiet and serene – until closing time. Then, the effect of local cider, known affectionately as scrumpy, is potent enough to send people home singing lustily, parting with a slightly slurred "So long".

The last vintage train puffed off to Glastonbury some years ago, and with it a little piece of Victorian Wells pulled out for ever, to the sadness of all lovers of the little steam railways that were active in Somerset less than half a century ago.

The commercial quarter remains on the Glastonbury and Wookey sides; on the other open country sweeps to the very walls of the Cathedral precincts, making Wells almost unique. To appreciate this uniqueness the city should be approached at least once on foot across the fields from Dulcote. From the Shepton Mallet road where the lane slopes upwards soon after leaving the village is a wicket gate on the left under a spreading tree. A properly made-up path leads into broad cornfields sloping down from the Mendips, where all is peace and bird songs. Then, as the path breasts a rise, grey towers and pinnacles appear, half hidden by wooded hills. Soon the Cathedral is seen whole; mature trees and grazing cattle vie with the Palace turrets and battlements in creating a picture like no other in the Kingdom, a Cathedral and a Palace where the countryside comes to their very walls. Indeed, it is like nowhere in Europe either; Milan Cathedral faces a bare paved square, Cologne is the heart of a teeming city, Notre Dame at least has the Seine to set it off, but there are no cows or cornfields in Paris. Only Ely and St. Albans to my knowledge have meadows within sight, but neither has a moated Palace as perfection added to perfection.

A single day's tour allows only a fleeting glimpse of the most dominating features of many-sided Wells. A weekend gives in addition early morning peace and evening strolls round the placid moat into the scented fields, but even a week is hardly enough to peer into the countless little secrets it keeps hidden even from those who think they know it well.

Many of the thousands flocking in every year realise the need to return for a closer look at this Medieval jewel that has interest even in its paving stones, a city of contradictions where the Church towers above everything yet looks down tolerantly on holiday amusements in its own territory. There is much more to Wells than singing choirboys and swans that ring for their supper.

Wookey Hole

H. G. and the Hag

SERMONS down the centuries have preached the inadvisability of following a life qualifying oneself for a long sojourn Down Below. Secular pictures of the nether regions have long painted an equally unpleasant existence chivied by pickfork-bearing demons and too hot for comfort.

Readers feeling a little uncertain as to their ultimate destinations may be interested to know that from a leafy Somerset lane near Wells is the pleasantest possible route to Hell, through a deep forested ravine and a garden that was bright with tulips, wallflowers and blossoming shrubs last time I strolled along it en route to Hell's Ladder and the Underworld.

Hell's Ladder at Wookey Hole, a flight of damp stone steps of doubtful date, inhabited by bats and sundry other crawlies, leads to one of the oldest known habitations of humanity, and to the supreme puzzle of Mendip: where does the River Axe go between plunging into a swallet close to its source and reappearing at the entrance to Wookey Hole, only about three miles away, no less than eighteen hours later? Eighteen hours is a long time for a rushing young river to wander around under the earth. The discoveries being made by cave divers penetrating farther and farther into the inner chambers of Wookey only serve to intensify the puzzle; twenty have been explored at the time of writing, but they account only for a small section of the Axe's mysterious underground journey, proving that for every wonder opened to the public and the many more mapped and investigated by speleologists there must be another hidden miracle within the Mendip rocks. The old explanation why people climb mountains – because they are there – doubtless applies also to dangerous water-filled unknown cave systems that may reveal a miracle of nature beyond the next bend.

Ordinary visitors see the Axe, so to speak, the wrong way round, not where it plunges into the bowels of the Mendips and disappears, but where it emerges after its mystery tour from under a low rock arch. Steps on the right, just before the cave entrance, lead to a viewing platform where the river can be seen rushing out of its long imprisonment into the daylight of a forested ravine that keeps most of its wildness despite the car-parks and cafés only five minutes' walk away.

The Mendips are riddled with caves, being limestone hills, some of the best known and most negotiable being open to the public at Cheddar and Wookey Hole. The latter has the advantage in that it is approached by shady lanes not as yet overcrowded with traffic, and that the entrance to the caves is by footpath only and not direct from the road. The short stroll first through the flower garden and then alongside a deep valley is a peaceful prelude to the descent of Hell's Ladder and a meeting with the Witch of Wookey.

Guides at the caves say that the two most frequently asked questions are, how long have the caves been known, and was there really a witch? Despite having to rattle off the same commentary to scores of parties composed of six gawpers to one truly interested person, those young men and women manage to make the tour amusing as well as informative, trying to answer the two stock questions as though they had never been asked before.

The caves, the guides will repeat, were accessible to wild beasts and possibly primitive people about 60,000 years ago, as excavations have proved. Many were now extinct creatures: the giant mammoth, cave lions, rhinoceros, wolves, deer, wild horses and others. The hyaenas apparently had the upper hand by their ruthless hunting habits, roaming in hungry packs and, by primitive animal reasoning, driving their prey towards the cliff edge, where the hunted crashed to mutilation or death to become food for the hunters; many broken bones have been found in this hyaenas' slaughter yard.

Scientific exploration revealed the strange fact that Wookey Hole was occupied several times alternately by men and by hyaenas, though nobody has as yet fully explained how either group periodically drove the other out and took possession.

Inside the main entrance are good examples of the rock found here, called conglomerate or, more unscientifically, pudding-stone. It was in the outer parts that man was found to have dwelt in the very dim past, in completely different conditions to the open-air life of the marshland lake-village folk. Here people lived in damp darkness, fashioning their simple tools and eking out an existence with wild beasts. Fascinating evidence has been found; grindstones and even a little wheat; hearthstones, and remains of joints of meat. It is sometimes added, with a certain relish, that human bones were found, intimating that the inhabitants may have had a cannibal tendency. Less gruesome are their tools, combs and ornaments, on show in a small museum.

The wonders of nature underground are small as well as awesome; no plant life had ever grown here until electric lights were installed; soon afterwards bright green ferns and fronds appeared, growing from seeds that had seeped through from the earth far above, to come to life when given light and warmth. Many of the lamps have these delicate groups of ferns around them, plants that have never seen the sky.

On the visitors go, to descend the chilly Ladder to see one of the miracles of underground Mendip (incidentally, it pays to see the caves early in the day or out of season, with a small and truly attentive party, rather than join the tourist mob and fight to see while missing half the very instructive commentary).

Deep down the passage opens into the breathtaking chamber where broods the Witch of Wookey over a scene of astonishing beauty and colour: yes, colour, far from the light of day, made visible to ordinary people by electric light. The light, it will be pointed out, is white, and not coloured, throwing up the genuine shades of nature from the gloom. Through the cave flows the River Axe, a deep blue-green and apparently very quiet and serene. This is an illusion; the river flows fairly fast, showing how far it must have wandered and circled inside the hills during the eighteen long hours since it left Priddy such a short distance away. A small boat is drawn up on a miniature sandy beach. Looking down on the river is the huge formation called the Witch of Wookey, silhouetted in shadow to show the hooked nose, haggish profile, and protuberant bust.

The legend of the Witch is an ancient one, and some very descriptive handed-down verses were known by heart to most of my own schoolmates, and doubtless still are. The "blear-eyed hag" turned her evil eyes on crops, young lovers, and local farmers with such ill will that eventually a deputation went to the Abbot of Glastonbury begging him to rid them of the menace. He duly dispatched a monk who drove the witch into the inner cave, sprinkled holy water over her, and "Lo, where stood a hag before, now stood a ghastly stone", the stone called the Witch of Wookey. All Medieval folklore and romancing? So it was assumed until a discovery in 1912 that, like many other Somerset excavations, proved rather than disproved legend. There was some such inhabitant, whose skeleton was found with her dagger, sacrificial knife and a big rounded ball of pure white stalagmite, the witch's ball. Beside her were the skeletons (or "skellingtons" as my latest guide preferred to call them) of two goats tied to a stake, dying with the witch for lack of freedom to escape.

The Hall of Wookey is a marvel of colour, rising to a high narrow dome. Notwithstanding the selfishness of the poet Pope who shot down some of the glorious formations to decorate his private grotto when they were the fashionable rage, the chamber is grand and beautiful together. Numberless stalactites form curtains of pink, milk-white, pale grey and black. Ingenuity with the spotlight picks out a few amusing sidelights: the picture of St. Paul's in a group of white formations – or, to French visitors, a likeness of Sacré Coeur of Paris – and the witch's turkey, "the one she didn't have time to cook" before being turned to stone, the guides like to wisecrack.

The last chamber accessible to the public is the most extraordinary, an engineering feat in rock that could never, scientists say, stand unsupported if built by humanity. It is not unlike the dome of the Albert Hall, without the hall underneath, a gigantic chamber over 130 feet across but nowhere above ten feet high; at the edges, the dome curves even lower almost to the floor. It is a spooky place, where the river comes from under a low arch, marking the limit beyond which only divers and aqualung enthusiasts can penetrate. Cave divers, we are told, have so far entered another 17 chambers from here, and far from coming to an end only find more to be investigated – and still they cannot explore far enough to discover exactly where the Axe loses itself during those mysterious forgotten hours.

It is here that Wookey's famous noises are heard, very rarely and by few, sounds that were apparently heard by the ancient writer Clement of Alexandria in the 2nd century, who likened them to crashing cymbals. They are caused when the river, swollen in flood, is trapped in the chamber under the far arch, where air is compressed and then thrown out under pressure into the big cavern. Starting with the distinctive cymbal sounds, the eerie din is said to rise to a horrifying crescendo when the pent up flood bursts foaming from the inner caves.

Wookey Hole

Wookey Hole has an awesomeness that in some respects outdoes Cheddar's two spectacular cave systems and also the benefit of that refreshing return through forested glades and a garden to the starting point, alongside one of the paper mills for which Wookey is famous. One has been long noted for its production of very high quality handmade notepapers.

Now a national nature reserve with signposted trails, created in memory of Sir Winston Churchill, Ebbor Gorge effectively suggests Cheddar's probable appearance before the first highway brought the first trippers. Altogether some 100 acres are now managed and protected from commercial spoliation.

Wookey entered literary history on the day a certain new master, "Bertie" Wells, arrived at its little Gothic village school, only a lad himself, possessed of an easy facility with the sketching pencil, a consuming passion for reading, and no idea of his future career.

Meanwhile he who would be known to posterity simply as H. G. Wells must earn his keep somehow. His mother, a stern and organising woman, had conveniently remembered a remote cousin, headmaster of the National School at Wookey; could he find a berth for her bright but undecided boy? Would Bertie make a teacher?

Unknown to Mother, however, the head was himself unqualified for his post, having forged papers and references to get the job. The rather charming rogue was now waiting with a certain relish for authority to rumble him.

The young H. G. Wells began as a pupil-teacher, barely older than his own class at the age of fourteen. His career lasted only the three months it took the National Schools' powers to catch up with the imposter head, who with his youthful assistant teacher was forthwith removed from the school and from the cottage that went with the post. So ended the brief career in this Somerset backwater of the man who was to become one of the acknowledged giants of English literature.

H.G. and a vindictive hag are the sort of oddly matched pair one might half expect in Somerset of the unexpected, along with cavemen living in hyaena-haunted caverns while their neighbours were living in the completely opposite conditions of the marshes and the open sky. What a pity the author did not, so far as can be ascertained, write a book involving some of those fascinating people whose lives were stranger than fiction.

Cheddar Gorge.

Cheddar
Alfred and the Archangel

12

Queue for this, queue for that; peer over shoulders to see nothing; tramping feet trailing a guide too far ahead to be heard; rushing past sights that need a long gaze; emerging into the sunlight to queue again for snacks or places at the tea-table before dashing along a jammed road to a waiting coach, too intent on self-preservation among the traffic to lift up eyes to the hills: for far too many, this is a picture of Cheddar on a Sunday or Bank Holiday in summer. Wearily, they drive off after seeing a few floodlit stalactites and the first few yards of the celebrated Gorge, sensing that they have somehow missed the real Cheddar. And they have.

It need not be so, if only people thought; this loveliest of villages can and should be seen in its spectacular setting with babbling streams running by, not avoided for fear that crowds will ruin its beauty or motor engines drown the birds and brooks. The answer is in two words: thoughtful planning, the operative word being thoughtful. Study maps, timetables and road routes, think a little about the herd habits of humanity, and there is no reason why Cheddar should not be seen pleasantly even at weekends, simply by dividing the days into, three phases. Arrive early when the Gorge is quiet and walkable and the caves uncrowded, abandon both between lunchtime and teatime for lesser-lauded corners not necessarily appearing in the guide books, and return to the centre after the last coaches have gone, when late afternoon shadows increase nature's drama to its climax, filling the chasm until only the topmost pinnacles still catch the sinking sun while roosting birds wheel around them, and see dusk become scented night in the Cheddar Gorge the coach parties have left behind them, the true Cheddar.

Instead of joining a tour, tied to a rigid schedule, it is much more worthwhile to catch instead an early bus, or drive out straight from breakfast, arriving in the near silence of the new day while mist wreathes and softens the peaks into Corot-like delicacy without diminishing their grandeur. I did it once from Weston, stepping off in supposedly tourist-jammed Cheddar to find myself alone with the birds. The only sounds were of trickling water and the occasional Somerset-accented voice: and this was July, the height of the season. And the time? Ten to nine on a midweek morning. Cheddar looked unbelievably lovely, old stone cottages huddling in the Gorge under the sheer cliffs, in a world of palest greens, blues and greys, where fuchsias dangled over running brooks, and a few cyclists and walkers had the famous ravine to themselves.

It is often quite late in the morning before visitors arrive in real numbers, so an early start allows for a leisurely stroll along roads that would be suicidal a few hours later. At one time walkers and traffic shared the same narrow grey-walled road to the caves, but a bypass footpath now takes pedestrians by a beautiful wooded route starting near the bridge over the little stream at the beginning of the Gorge. Thus walkers can linger, and look down on the lovely clear lake reflecting the scenery above, whose waters are so fresh that the bottom can be seen far out in its centre. The lake feeds a waterfall, formerly only visible from the rear gardens of the Cliff Hotel – though it is still worth patronising that establishment for the even better view of the fine fall with Cheddar cliffs beyond. If there is anything pleasanter than lingering along this new tree-lined path on a summer morning, nibbling scones and rolls bought while still warm from the oven, with only robins for company, it must be good indeed.

The part around the lake and its little river is one of the most charming corners of Cheddar for those wise enough to arrive in the quiet of the day; in spring it is even lovelier, when prunus blossom adds its myriad bunches of pale pink rose-like clusters to the greens and greys of the Gorge. The footpath emerges at the farther end of the lake, near the biggest cave system, but it is worthwhile first to walk back a little on the road itself, viewing the Lion Rock that glowers like a reclining beast above some picturesquely placed cottages, his nose a little flattened as though in battle, but otherwise remarkably lion-like. It is an interesting photographic or painters' study, this creature sculpted by winds and weather; as well as the picture-postcard view in sunshine, there is the harder silhouette against back-lighting, the lion at dusk or dawn, or snoozing under a gentle grey

Cheddar - the sound of water is always in the air.

drizzle; the drama of the Lion Rock is for the expressive brush or creative photographer rather than the holiday snapshotter.

Cottages straggle higgledy-piggledy under Cheddar cliffs, not the true village but a more familiar offshoot of it. Many are now cafés or souvenir shops; the sensitive may sneer at commercialism if they will, but Cheddar's souvenir shops have a certain attraction of their own adding to the prettiness of the scene rather than detracting from it. They sell all the usual trinkets and cards, naturally, but there are also local sheepskin rugs. Many inevitably sell Cheddar cheese and cream, though the genuine cottage article has been largely superseded, so far as the mass market is concerned, by commercial varieties, sold in individual rounds at various weights. Zummerzet zider comes in blatantly souvenir pottery containers, snapped up as ornaments but not containing a lot of booze. As a drink, the plainer and larger bottles seem a better bargain – but do not under-estimate the power of what some people imagine is almost as teetotal as lemonade; cider has a kick, as closing time at a village bar will confirm.

Is it to be the caves first, or the Gorge? This is the obvious question on meeting with the entrance to the first and tantalising views of the second from the same point, where the shops end. It is what countrymen call "six o' one and half-a-dozen o' t'other", both being at their best as early as possible.

For open-air characters on a fine morning, the Gorge invariably wins, when it is possible to share it with walkers and climbers and a minimum of traffic. Turning the first bend past the caves leaves little choice – the views ahead draw the walker onwards as surely as a Svengali drawing a lesser mortal to himself by the hypnotic power of his personality. Every step shows a new vista of this finest stretch of the Gorge, that simply must be covered on foot if it is to be seen whole. Sadly, the majority of tourist parties view little of it, being deposited near the caves and finding time only for a quick look round the first couple of bends afterwards before driving on, this being but one reason why Cheddar is better visited by bus or car without the ties of limited time. A whole day could easily be spent in the Gorge. Walking through its grandest parts before noon traffic builds up, each twist brings a better angle, until the road squeezes between limestone cliffs towering sheer to close on 500ft. Birds eternally wheel and cry round the dizzy rock pinnacles, where fly-small human figures dangle from seemingly fragile ropes, scaling the challenging walls of stone.

Last time I saw Cheddar Gorge, I had not long returned from the fantastic ravines of the mighty Dolomites; Cheddar at first appeared to have shrunk, in comparison with those awesome jagged ranges, but after a few minutes' walk its old power to thrill asserted itself. Cheddar was not the Dolomites, but on the other hand neither were the Dolomites Cheddar; this English canyon soon regained its perspective of grandeur as laid against its own country's landmarks.

Certainly nowhere in England is quite like the Gorge for photography; every angle is magnificent, particularly looking across a bend rather than ahead, allowing for the fact that the sun striking head-on has a diminishing effect while shadows on the rock faces accentuate their size. Altogether the main Gorge from the caves twists and turns for about two miles of superb rock scenery, the finest part being the first half mile or so up to the well-named Horseshoe Bend. Farther up the road gradually climbs and the scenery becomes less awesome though still rugged and rocky. Up here the bulk of the tourists rarely penetrate, thanks to their timetables, but there are limitless corners for the unfettered holidaymaker to camp and picnic while the crowds take over the popular parts for the afternoon. After about two miles the road makes a large turn on itself towards Priddy, while a little-known footpath leads ahead to Velvet Bottom and

Mendip Top near historic Charterhouse, another sheltered refuge from the motoring throng.

Cheddar Gorge has always fascinated the daring, from schoolboys teetering on slippery paths to nowhere, to elaborately equipped rock climbers. Tales are told of high-wire walkers attempting to cross the broad ravine, and of huntsmen and hounds galloping towards the brink to plunge over to destruction after the fox. Once in a while someone thinks of a new stunt, such as an attempt to jump on a specially built motor cycle across the yawning gap.

One of the best ways to see the Gorge without crowds is to go there on a Bank Holiday: a normal Bank Holiday, that is, namely wet. I tried it only last year, in nothing but a mild soft drizzle, and was astonished to find that, to paraphrase Churchill, rarely were so many kept away by so harmless a drop of moisture. Only the occasional car cruised by, and long periods of perfect peace reigned over what should have been a trippers' takeover. It seemed unbelievable that so soft and warm a West Country drizzle could make it possible to walk farther than ever before up Cheddar Gorge on a Bank Holiday, followed by tours of both sets of caves without waiting to enter, another example of how it pays to study the habits of the tourist majority and plan accordingly.

It is not always gentle rain that falls on Cheddar, as anyone familiar with Somerset will realise; as remarked once before, when it rains it rains. Being caught in a thunderstorm is one of the most unforgettable experiences possible, once a sheltered nook has been found; thunder crashes and reverberates around the echoing rocks whose wet surfaces magnify and spread the rumble, while the rain splatters noisily on hard rock walls and trees bending in the winds trapped in a natural wind-tunnel. A local clergyman wrote the hymn "Rock of Ages" while sheltering from such a tempest in Burrington Combe, a lesser Mendip ravine; nowhere is it more significant than in Cheddar Gorge while thunder bellows round and round towering rain-lashed peaks.

The same principle applies when touring Cheddar's two publicly shown cave systems as applies to the Gorge: choose the right time, not the peak of the afternoon, and marvel with a small party where 400 feet of solid rock stand over your head while miracles of underground colour are before you. Gough's are the larger of the two, where the skeleton called Cheddar Man was found, a man believed to have lived 10,000-12,000 years ago. There is no sinister Hell's Ladder here, only a civilised descending pathway; as at Wookey, delicate fern fronds live around the lamp bulbs, brought to life by the heat and light replacing the sun of a world they have never seen.

Gough's Caves have some of the finest limestone formations of Cheddar, the stalactites, stalagmites, grottoes and curtains peculiar to limestone caves. The Fonts is a series of basins apparently overflowing with palest pink and green water that is really lime and its mineral contents. Somewhere beneath is an underground river, whose course is uncharted; some surmise that it could be the lost Axe which turns up at Wookey Hole after a mysterious 18-hour underground journey, but this is pure guesswork. However, at least one local yarn supports the supposition; one day a stray dog wandered into Cheddar Caves, below which this river certainly runs, to reappear at Wookey Hole – shorn of every hair. Geologists allow that the tortuous underground stream must negotiate eddies, cataracts confined to narrow passages, and foaming waterfalls; their force could conceivably "shave" a loose haired breed, already in the moulting season. Additionally, dogs are noted for their remarkable footing on surfaces we cannot scale, and for their powers of survival. Only by throwing himself into this uncharted subterranean labyrinth without protective headgear could humanity prove or disprove the river's efficiency as a razor, as demonstrated in the story of the dog. For what it is worth, it can be pointed out that this is not a current tall tale for credulous visitors, but was circulated generations before the tourist invasion. Occasionally the river rises in flood to fill the caves, burst through the entrance, and rush down the street; photographs of the flood show cars inundated to the headlights in swirling water making the village street a river.

The cave guides tell that experiments over three decades show that stalactites and stalagmites take as much as 4,000 years to grow one single cubic inch, formed by rainwater seeping through from the earth above, carrying lime; the evaporated water leaves a minute extra deposit of lime on the growing formation. A favourite group is the Swiss Village, caused by reflections in a still pool, resembling fields and hedges with a tiny church on a hill. Sometimes visitors are allowed to touch a solid mass of lime like a huge nightlight in shape, and try to assimilate the fact that it took 30,000 years to grow; the mind cannot truly comprehend so vast a span.

One of the highlights is Solomon's Temple, which Solomon in all his glory could not have created as have minute drops of rain over thousands of years, a mass of hanging curtains from palest green to pure white; suddenly the lights are snapped off, and from the pitch blackness dawn breaks and the sun rises until the Temple is flooded with light from the Organ Pipes formation to one's feet. Niagara Falls, too, have an underground namesake, reputedly half a million years old. In Cheddar's case the brilliantly conceived floodlighting does not cheapen nature's work but reveals its full wonder.

It was near Solomon's Temple that one strong-nerved man lived for 130 days in an inner pit 90ft deep, to establish a record for staying alone, in deep hollow, and came up comparatively well after his ordeal.

The entire cave is a succession of miracles in petrified stone and mineral, sometimes spreading like the wing of a vast bird or angel; it is not mere fancy that entitles one of the best to be called the Archangel's Wing, for so glorious a formation could only be associated with the highest. One thing stumps many people almost as much as stretching their imaginations to take in ages counted in tens of thousands of years: what is the difference between a stalagmite and a stalactite? The valuable art of mnemonics usefully links them in rhyme: "Mites like mountains, tites like fountains", meaning that stalagmites rise from the floor as mountains rise from the earth, while stalactites hang downwards like the spray falling back from a fountain. A useful alliterative alternative picks out the "c" and "g" in the two words: "c" for stalactite (they hang from the ceiling), and "g" for stalagmites (rising from the ground).

Explorers who do not suffer from either claustrophobia or aching feet should not miss Cox's Caves after having seen Gough's; they are quite different and, though the smaller, are generally considered the more beautiful in their fairylike grottoes. The entrance is lower down into the village. Here too colour is in the rock: green of copper, grey of lead, pink of iron, and white of lime. Again, clever lighting increases the impact, as when the party arrives in a dark cavern to gasp audibly when the lights are switched on. Those who have seen it all before still feel that catch of the breath as the miraculous beauty created by tiny drops of rain is revealed. Another cavern has marble-like formations resembling a swept-up theatre curtain, folded and draped like fabric. One set of lime blocks is called The Bells, producing different notes when hit; the guides like to tap out such tunes as "Come to the cookhouse door, boys" on them. The water grottoes are outstandingly beautiful for their reflections of natural miracles in miniature.

After a morning of what the local wags call cave-bashing, treat yourself to an early lunch in a cottage garden. Meals outdoors were a

Cheddar pleasure long before Continental ideas began to infiltrate into our indoor-dining land. Even during the last war, when tourists were few, Somerset people going there for the day enjoyed fully cooked lunches outdoors with the looming cliffs as shelter. Things have altered little since, though more sophisticated eating places have grown up nearby. Solidly unadventurous beef, spuds and carrots in a cottage garden tastes as good as a banquet indoors. Alternatively, it is fun to buy a punnet of luscious freshly picked monster strawberries and a pot of cream, and sneak into a rocky corner for a snack; such pleasure cannot be recommended for the figure, but it does no harm.to indulge so gluttonously just once, and there is still the afternoon to walk off the effects.

The main Gorge is best left to the trippers after lunch, the bulk of the coaches arriving between about noon and 3 p.m., but that need not mean retreating altogether; a different viewpoint is enough. A little-explored track on the lower Gorge's northern flank, rising behind a couple of prettily placed cottages, leads to wide, wild views that are not shown on the postcards, as well as peace. I have spent a whole afternoon up there watching the human ants and toytown cars that give the scene its perspective, in company only with butterflies. Bold gaunt cliffs rear starkly black against the sun's glare; sombre greens, blues and greys colour the rich vegetation; heavy shadows are pierced by dramatic shafts of sunshine.

Another escape to the hilltops is offered by Jacob's Ladder, but it is worthwhile first seeing a third cave. This Waterfall Cave, near the foot of the Ladder, looks like a cleverly contrived source of extra revenue at first, natural waters being channelled into formal sprays and completed with changing coloured lighting. The true fall is reached through a second short passage, where it can be heard roaring and thundering through the closely confined rock chambers. I had met waterfalls inside mountains before, in Switzerland and in Italy, but never before in England: this specimen compared favourably, plunging downwards inside the rock through a chimney-like crevice cut by never-ceasing water pouring from some hidden stream above. The noise was deafening in the enclosed space, and the flying spray meant keeping cameras under cover, as the fall leapt down and disappeared into some underground pool in boiling foam.

Wookey Hole and Cheddar have one striking difference: at Wookey a spooky damp ladder leads into the bowels of the earth and Hell; at Cheddar another flight of steps ascends the open cliffside to Heaven, or at least in the right direction. Jacob's Ladder, a muscle-murdering stairway up the sheer face, attracts an active minority, leading to new vistas and clear sunny air; for cowards, narrow lanes approach the hilltop from behind the cliffs. The climb is long and stiff, but the panoramas from the top are worth the effort. From the brink of precipitous cliffs the road looks like a ribbon far below, and footpaths follow the edge towards the sheerest and highest points above the famous chasm. In the opposite direction there are open views towards Glastonbury Tor, Axbridge Lake, the moors, and the coast.

An entire afternoon is not too long to wander at random here on the top of the Mendips, possibly hoping to spot the rare Cheddar Pink, from which a local perfume is made. Naturalists who know its whereabouts are not anxious to divulge the secret, to protect the uncommon little plant. The Cheddar Pink (dianthus gratianopolitanus), a relative of the ordinary wild pink, grows from clusters of thin spiky blue-green leaves on a fragile hair-like stalk, and is native only to Cheddar's limestone rocks.

The pale pink petals lie open almost flat, whereas the commoner variety's petals turn slightly upwards and are more ragged at the edges and paler. Another locally named plant is the Cheddar whitebeam (sorbus anglica) of the mountain ash family. It is found also on limestone hills in Devon and the Welsh border country, but its close cousin, sorbus wilmottiana, is peculiar only to the wooded parts of Cheddar Gorge. This shrub has bright green leaves and clusters of perky little white flowers not unlike pear blossom, with shiny red berries in autumn. While on the subject of dry sunny hilltops, it is worth remembering that adders are fond of such country; they are commoner on the topmost hills and near bracken, where "Danger, Adder Warning" is occasionally seen on hillside gates, but they are sometimes met above Cheddar as well.

Cheddar is two distinct villages, the scattered cottages in the Gorge and the true village about a mile south, the two being separated by the aptly named Tweentown. The main village is of considerable charm, a dreamy sprawl of grey stone houses. There is a good specimen of the arched and covered village cross, and a number of imposing properties, a reminder that tourist Cheddar is comparatively new while the older village was in existence centuries earlier when, like Axbridge, it was once patronised by the Royal chase when kings hunted over the Royal Forest of Mendip.

Hannah More, the 18th-century reformer who laboured so hard to improve social conditions in the district, was inspired to intensify her campaign by Cheddar's squalor at that time. She made her working headquarters in a Cheddar cottage that became, in continuance of her work for the public good, the local Red Cross and old people's centre.

The church, half buried in dark trees and so far from the Gorge that it is missed by many tourists, is a sample of the Somerset Perpendicular style. As in most rural communities, church and village are closely knit together; in the vicarage garden I remember a wonderful evening of old fashioned country dancing on the lawns, a whirl of coloured skirts and flying ribbons, as local youth danced until dark. The two sisters running the house where I was staying treated their guests like friends, and worked hours any city union would have found incredible. At midnight the smell of boiling ham, smoking bacon or freshly made jam floated from the kitchen, before the good ladies retired to bed up an outside staircase, carrying flickering lanterns.

During excavations for a new school in the village, one of the decade's most important archaeological discoveries was made, the remains of an Anglo-Saxon palace mentioned in King Alfred's will. Alfred had already made history only a few miles away in bringing about the Peace of Wedmore, but this find in Cheddar helped fill some of the gaps in our knowledge of his life and building methods. It had been occupied during four different periods from the reign of Ethelwulf onwards, as coins found on the site tell. When the school, suitably named the Kings of Wessex School, was completed the gardens were landscaped to show and preserve the remains of the palace. Somehow, one can imagine King Alfred being pleased rather than pained to find parts of his Cheddar home incorporated into a modern school, having been in his time an exceptional scholar, historian and educationalist, keen to improve his people's minds as well as to protect them from such enemies as the Danes. A few miles away at Winthill the keen archaeological group has also found another precious Saxon relic, an engraved glass bowl that proved to be a rare and valuable specimen. It is preserved in the Ashmolean Museum at Oxford where the Alfred jewel, found near his Athelney camp, is also on show; thus two of the best relics so far found of the brave and wise King Alfred repose in the same building.

Going off into the country is yet another way of passing the hours while Cheddar Gorge is overcrowded, and of discovering how Cheddar lives, apart from tourism. Cheddar cheese was the main cottage and farm industry until last century, and continues now on a small scale, but most of it is now mass produced to a similar recipe.

A minor pursuit is the making of cheese straws. Of greater value today are the strawberry fields between here and Draycott, producing lush and large berries on the rich but well-drained hillsides with the clear western sun to ripen them and gentle western rain to swell them. Polythene is used for protection, laid in tubes like outsized shining worms basking side by side.

Farm life is all around you on the Mendips; following a random path often leads to the making of a pleasant passing friendship with a sow and her piglets or a chat with a couple of farm horses; country folk know the genuinely interested visitor from the trespasser, and can be very friendly and informative to those showing real interest in their farms. I have had such an episode end with the pleasure of a lift in an old-world trap or governess-cart behind a trotting horse, those charming means of transport being not as yet entirely extinct.

To the charm of the Somerset hills, incidentally, a great continent across the world owes its most notorious agricultural problem – the rabbit of Australia. Early in the 19th century a Somerset couple recently settled in Tasmania found themselves missing only one thing in that otherwise delightful country, the homely Somerset bunny. So deeply did thy miss his cheerful presence that they had two dozen English rabbits shipped out, to live initially like pets. Rabbits being rabbits, the two dozen became hundreds. A population explosion obviously being imminent, the Tasmanians set about thinning the rabbits by sending some over to the Australian mainland, as yet rabbit free; there they were joined by others imported by another homesick immigrant. Within five years the innocent two dozen had become thirty thousand, whose descendants laughed in armies at men, dogs, poisons, guns and fencing, eating crops and trees over vast areas. All because one ex-Somerset couple missed the charm of a Mendip rabbit.

Beyond the last houses, across the track of the old disused railway, is a Cheddar the average tourist to the famous caves and cliffs must surely not dream exists, a Cheddar without hills and as flat as any tabletop. Abruptly all the grandeur has disappeared, and the Moor has begun, part of the flat heartland of Somerset that was sea bed when the landlocked lagoon came to within a mile of the Mendip scarp-face. Suddenly you are back in the world of straight silver rhynes lined with lovely marsh plants, tall reeds and bulrushes, where coloured dragonflies hover like tiny helicopters over rhythmically swaying grasses. The only boundary is the sky where it meets infinity, and the only traffic has four cows' feet instead of four wheels. This is a side of Cheddar the tourists do not see, unfortunately for them, but of immense interest to naturalists, photographers and painters; if you love limitless space and would attempt to interpret the sky with a brush dipped in every shade of translucent blue, spare time for the moors as well as the cliffs. Standing lately by a rhyne, I was reminded of a favourite lesson in acquiring a sensitive ear for sound preached by that supreme musician and lover of the country, Sir Adrian Boult. Stand motionless, shut your eyes, and listen to the silence. Silence? Closed eyes bring the outdoor world into sharp focus, as well as music, and it is amazing how many noises there are in a supposedly remote field: humming bees, a cow lowing distantly, a farm dog, a car's horn, wind brushing stiff reeds, rattling seed pods, a child's voice, a fish surfacing for food, two birds arguing over the same crumb. It is an interesting exercise in truly hearing and identifying the small sounds of the fields, as well as in concentration.

And so back to Cheddar when the last coachloads have departed; by about 6 p.m. its true face is showing again. Evening is the most impressive time of all in Cheddar, when the shadows are as dramatic as the rocks that create them; gradually peace descends, but for running water and sleepy birds. Shade fills the deep ravine with ghostly greys while the lowering sun touches the highest crags with a last kiss of gold. The Horseshoe Bend, a natural amphitheatre where the Gorge twists round a half circle, is particularly striking at nightfall. Like the Cheddar of early morning, the village, the farmlands and the moorlands, the Cheddar of dusk is a sight the tourists leave behind them.

The Gorge and the caves, impressive though they are, make up only a part of the entire Cheddar, which needs far more than a day excursion for full exploration. There are enough facets of this crown jewel of Somerset to occupy a week's holiday; then there will be time to see it from all angles and in all lights, to seek out the latest discovery from the days of King Alfred, and to choose the best time to go under ground and gaze on an Archangel's Wing that is separated from Heaven by 400 feet of solid, miracle-creating Mendip limestone rock.

Axbridge

Saxon Kings and Strawberries

13

AXBRIDGE was old a thousand years ago, old enough indeed to be a Borough by the reign of Edward the Confessor. It lies beneath the Mendips, set between those lovely hills and a wide lake, surrounded by the strawberry beds for which the area is now famous, and from which much of the little town's prosperity comes.

Though Cheddar is within walking distance, few of the visitors thronging that spectacular village find their way to its ancient neighbour. Yet, centuries before Cheddar was invaded by tourists, Axbridge was often invaded by groups of gorgeously dressed and splendidly mounted knights, followers of the royal hunts of the Anglo-Saxon and Norman kings. The king himself rode at their head.

Until well into the 17th century the Mendips were royal hunting country, where the king alone, with his retainers and followers, had the right to hunt the stags roaming the hills. In practice, His Majesty's rights were not entirely respected locally, for poaching was itself a popular sport, carried out with considerable ingenuity despite the severe penalties dealt out to those who were inevitably caught in the act.

Axbridge was the chief base for the hunting over the Royal Forest of Mendip; in Anglo-Saxon and Norman days in particular, stag-hunting there was the goodly sport of several monarchs.

Clattering hooves often broke the sleepy silence when a colourful hunting party, tired and thirsty from the chase, descended into the village for refreshments, wine and merriment, at the expense of the local burgesses. Those gentlemen found themselves faced with the unenviable choice of unbalancing their finances, or offending a hungry king.

Westcountry History: Somerset

King John's Hunting Lodge in Axbridge.

King John's name is still spoken, for a picturesque old house commanding the entry to the small square is known as King John's Hunting Lodge despite its very apparent Elizabethan construction. Almost certainly the name has been handed down from an earlier building on the same site, as King John frequented the Mendips as a huntsman. When the Lodge's overhanging frontage was restored, traces of earlier work were revealed underneath it. Eventually the hidden Elizabethan facade was revealed in its dilapidated timbered beauty. Restoration was of necessity heavy and drastic; nevertheless the redecorated and renovated building is extremely striking, more so than before the cleaning and repairs.

The days when monarchs galloped into the streets and horns echoed over the hills were occasionally re-enacted in the Axbridge Pageant, a wonderful historical spectacle. The first was given in 1967. The scenes, brought to life in the picturesque streets, have an impact no artificial theatrical setting could impart, the stamp of reality.

In the second Pageant 250 people plus horses and countless conveyances and properties recreated highlights of Axbridge's story from Roman times to the 20th century, the script being carefully based on the town's own comprehensive archives. Cowed Britons trudged through the Square driven by Roman overlords, on their way to work as slaves at the lead mines, followed by horse-drawn chariots driven by elaborately costumed Romans; King Edmund rode in with his attendants to beg Dunstan's forgiveness for a previous slighting, making him Abbot of Glastonbury; King John of course appeared, coming in with his huntsmen and courtiers; a band of rebels cheerfully went off to join Monmouth, reappearing later limping and weary after the fiasco of Sedgemoor. The arrival of Charles I's Queen, Henrietta Maria, was one of the highlights; gorgeously dressed citizens awaited her when she rode proudly in wearing a wide brimmed hat and flowing cloak, followed by her retinue. The Pageant went on through a riotous Victorian wedding scene to the arrival of the horseless carriage, a vintage motor driven by elaborately dressed travellers.

As sheer spectacle the Axbridge Pageants were impressive events; more than entertainment, they revive authentically scenes of nineteen centuries of Mendip history.

Axbridge was at one time an important wool town, whose speciality was knitted stockings. There is still a look of Medieval prosperity about the buildings lining the long narrow street which twists and winds for over a mile. This is nowadays a sleepy-looking old thoroughfare, as befits such an ancient town, thanks to an idea blessed with the brilliance of simplicity: the adaptation of the former Cheddar Valley railway route into a by-pass road that happens, by the ready-made lie of the track, to be most conveniently placed. This takes the bulk of such traffic as is not directly concerned with Axbridge, making walking the corkscrew main street the pleasure it should be, though at weekends and holiday times shadows of the old jams may occasionally reappear on a smaller scale, when motorists trying to squeeze through constrained corners for a quick glance, instead of enjoying Axbridge an foot, become entangled with localised traffic. The driver of a milk-churn loaded lorry, or a tractor with a trailer, will not be hurried by the curses of a motoring townsman who has suddenly become bent on seeing the back of the place without imbibing its slower going charms; though most such loads now avoid the centre, the odd agricultural vehicle can still appear at an inconvenient moment. A couple of buses running in opposite directions complete the brief reminder of pre-by-pass Axbridge when the familiar crawl could be both infuriating and amusing, according to one's need to hurry or otherwise.

Prosperous though outward appearances were in the Axbridge that saw this long winding street's development, and richly though its merchants lived, the place apparently had a seamier side. Hannah More, the indefatigable pioneer of social reform in Somerset, whose efforts on behalf of the immortal souls of Mendip's sons of the soil took her into virtually every village in the district, was no more impressed with Axbridge than with the remoter hamlets. "A wretched, beggarly town" the righteous lady called it. Nor were its inhabitants' characters of the purest; it was, she reported, "all anarchy and malice".

It is difficult now to imagine this quiet and orderly old town being as offensive as Hannah More painted it, but then it is equally difficult to picture scenes of horrific cruelty in the name of sport, performed publicly with the blessing of both mayor and clergy. Yet the ancient sport of bull-baiting, if sport it can be called, was once one of the highlights of the year. It continued, incredibly, right up to the 19th century, being held each year on Guy Fawkes' Day.

The proceedings opened, rather inappropriately, with a civic church service, attended in suitably arrayed dignity by the Mayor and his Corporation, which was presumably designed as some kind of conscience-clearing exercise, performed in advance. This formality over, the grand bull-baiting began, for which the populace had gathered in excited anticipation in the Square. The unfortunate bull was released to career madly through the town pursued by yelping dogs and by shouting men armed with clubs, which they wielded with the gusto of blood-lust. The capture of the by-then frenzied beast was the beginning of the real "sport". First he was tethered to the heavy bull-anchor, which still survives as a memento of those atrocious days of revelry, there to be worried to death by howling dogs which were egged on by the shouts of the populace. The Spanish bull-fight of today seems almost restrained by comparison; cruel it undoubtedly is, but at least this is an organised cruelty governed by extremely strict rules and according to strict time limits. Theoretically the bull stands a chance of winning if the matador puts but one foot wrong. I have even seen the bull save his hide by refusing to fight, when he is driven unscathed from the ring. Axbridge's bull-baitings had no such refinements; the more savage and long-lasting the agony, the more the dogs shrieked and the more the men yelled, the better the bloodthirsty mob enjoyed the revolting spectacle. To avoid the possibility of boredom through repetition, the sports were sometimes also enlivened with badger-baiting, for which the creature was imprisoned in a barrel to be tormented by savage hounds. Such was November the Fifth in smiling Somerset.

Does such outwardly peaceful countryside sometimes bring out some perverse streak in human nature, that occasionally expresses itself in violence? Though crime is scarce, it still can take a macabre turn; such a case was the notorious Evil Eye murder, the tale of which is repeated with lurid variations though a decade or more has passed.

The chief livelihood of Axbridge and its surrounding villages is agriculture. Strawberries in particular have been its fortune. During the season almost every gate around Axbridge and nearby Draycott seems to announce "Strawberries for sale, fresh picked today". Who can resist the large, luscious scarlet fruits? Certainly not most of the passing motorists and walkers. A feast of a complete punnet of strawberries with a lashing of cream does nothing for the waistline, but is one of the joys of an early summer morning in this refreshing part of England.

The strawberry fields slope gently from the feet of the Mendips towards the open moors below. In vivid contrast to the rocky hills and the dark peaty moors, these slopes are of a Devon-like reddish brown, adding to the lovely colouring of green Somerset meadows and yellow buttercups. Field after field is in various stages of production, so as to extend the season as long as nature will allow. Some plants ripen in the open among straw; others are under long glass cloches, open or closed according to the degree of warmth and air required. Many strawberry crops are ripened today under polythene; the great fat tubes of glistening polythene rather resemble gigantic worms laid side by side, often as long as a football pitch. From a distance such a field looks like shining water in the sunlight. Sometimes the yield may even be too good; too many strawberries ripening within a short period makes it impossible to market them all. Unsold fruit may be burned on the ground to clear the field quickly. Then, the air is not only scented with flowers and the smells of the countryside. It reeks of hot strawberry jam. Delicious, but heartbreaking.

Zummerzet Zider is usually in evidence at Mendip area romps; "Yer tiz" and "Yer 'ee be", inns announce, advertising the heady drink that can be the undoing of the occasional headstrong tourist; the locals themselves are better aware of its strength. Scrumpy, the potent cider is called locally. It is interesting to note that the schoolboy art of apple stealing under a farmer's nose is known as scrumping as far away as Kent. This is an art as old as cider making itself; a little carving in nearby Wells Cathedral shows thieves stealing scrumpy apples and being caught.

All life around Axbridge and the Mendips is linked with the land. As well as strawberries there are potato growing, mushroom rearing, and dairying. The traditional Harvest Festival is of special meaning in the lovely Somerset churches, but this is by no means the end of the affair. There is usually a variety of merriments, including scrumpy drinking, to cheery but forgivable excess. Harvest really means something in farming country.

Axbridge also has its more sophisticated patrons, the yachtsmen and women who come for the exhilarating sailing on Axbridge Lake, which is a man-made reservoir a good mile across and a mile wide. It is typical of this paradoxical county that the very land that was once submerged by an inland sea which has gone should be partly given back to the water in artificial lakes. Two of them, the Blagdon and Chew Valley reservoirs, lie north of the Mendips, but the Axbridge lake is actually situated where the sea met the hills. Thus something of central Somerset's former appearance is restored. Looking across from Axbridge, we have some idea of the probable low outline of the Isle of Wedmore when seen across open water.

The present lake blends delightfully with the landscape, particularly when blue and white sails heel and turn like seabirds in the brisk breezes blowing straight off the Bristol Channel across the open moors. In the background rise the Mendips, with the distinctive Crook's Peak piercing the skyline. The Peak was one of the many beacons that once conveyed messages of danger approaching or past from hill to hill in fire. As recently as 1945 many of them were used again, when the news of victory was passed from hill to hill all over Somerset in a chain of bonfires. Nobody who saw them will ever forget the sight. A fuller description of that night of rural rejoicing appears in the chapter dealing with the Polden Hills.

The glory of Axbridge as a town is the church of St. John the Baptist, impressive even by Somerset standards, for the style known as "Som. Perp." or Somerset Perpendicular is one of the most glorious in English church-building. The towers with their characteristic open lacework parapets are peculiar to the central and northern parts of this county. Huish Episcopi near Langport, the most famous, was once shown in one of the series of commemorative stamps featuring British architecture that have become regular events in the philatelic calendar. This tower has a permanent place in stamp albums throughout the globe: such is the architectural merit of the Somerset Perpendicular. Among other outstanding examples are those of Dundry north of the Mendips (the builder remarked that this was the third of its kind, of which he had "now dun dree", hence its name) and of Axbridge. A steep flight of steps leads up from Axbridge Square to the lofty old church; such an upward flight is rather unusual in churches dedicated to St. John, which are more often entered by stepping down, in token of the saint's humility, that "John decreases while He increases". At the foot of the church steps are the so-called Fishponds, where Axbridge residents may draw water by right. The church interior is magnificent, yet one of the first things the visitor may notice on entering is a quite ordinary glass-fronted cupboard, fixed to the wall just inside the main door. Within will probably be a number of new loaves of bread, neatly arranged as if in a baker's shop window. The case is inscribed:

> 1690. Spearing's Gift. Four shillings per week in bread to be given to the second poor of Axbridge for ever to be paid out of the South Brent Estate.

This is known as the Bread Charity, created under the will of William Spearing of 1688. To qualify for a loaf of bread – a considerable treasure to the poor of the donor's time – the recipients had to attend morning service and to be truly "poor housekeepers" of the parish, receiving no public relief.

The nave ceiling of Axbridge church is of exceptional beauty, a masterpiece for which a local craftsman received the huge sum of ten guineas in 1636. Its restoration cost over £4,000. Now its glory shines afresh, a study in clear blue, white, and gold. Three great stone pendants hang like chandeliers of white and gold from the roof. Another treasure is the huge candelabrum above the chancel, of intricately designed brass, weighing well over a hundredweight.

Many changes have come to Axbridge over the centuries. The waters that lapped its shores have gone, leaving dairy pastures where the sea once lay; kings and nobles no longer crowd into its streets after the stag-hunt, though fox-hunting continued, by Mendip farmers instead of royalty; the wealthy merchants no longer trade from this ancient town; Guy Fawkes' Night means children's fireworks instead of savage bull-baiting in the Square. It is a peaceable place now, remembering the past while remaining self reliant through the strawberry trade that carries its name throughout England every summer.

Axbridge, however, is not dead. Dreaming it may be, but Axbridge's dreams are noble ones, as befits a former haunt of kings.

The South Face of the Mendips
Slaves and Sunday Schools

14

DEDUCT Wells, Wookey Hole, Cheddar and Axbridge from the Mendip gazetteer, and what remains? In mathematical terms, the answer should come close to nil, a string of unfamiliar villages and bare hills whose tops are an uninteresting-looking plateau. Sums do not always work out according to the tables, however, in paradoxical Somerset; in this instance, subtracting the four chief centres leaves enough minor interests to fill a chapter.

From the sea at Uphill the Mendips run some 25 miles inland, a long even stretch of upland having a character and history of its own. The hills are chiefly of limestone, hence their abundance of caves and swallet holes, with rich lead deposits that made them highly prized by the Romans. The Roman influence begins where the hills themselves start; at the ancient port near Uphill that was the terminus of the road from the lead mines.

Caves are the distinctive feature of limestone areas, and the Mendips are no exception; only three at Cheddar and one at Wookey Hole are open to the general public, but a large number of caves, swallets and potholes are regularly explored by the caving groups of the area, whose dangerous expeditions have a common lure; what lies inside the earth? It can safely be assumed that not all the hills' marvels have been discovered yet, though new caves naturally become more unlikely with today's enthusiastic group membership and efficient equipment; all the same, a major discovery is always possible under these hills that hide great beauty in their hearts. Loxton, one of the first villages of the main ridge, had caves of no less than ten chambers, all of exquisite natural beauty, but in the days when people helped themselves without thought of preservation or regard for others' pleasure, whole cartloads of stalactites and stalagmites were carried off. It might have been a second Wookey for this generation had the caves been left intact.

Where the road from Cheddar to Weston follows a gap in the hills is Winscombe, sprawling into a town thanks to the nearness of the sea that makes it a desirable residential area. Better known than the place is Sidcot School whose immaculately maintained playing fields can be seen from the roadside. The boarding school dates from the 18th century, and was founded, like many other public-spirited institutions in the county, by the Society of Friends or Quakers, being in its early days open only to children of Quaker families. From this point almost to Wells is the most interesting section, geographically and historically, and the part having the best scenery culminating in the mighty cleft of Cheddar Gorge.

Black Down is the highest point, at 1,067 feet above sea level, but the whole scarp-face of the range is equally notable for spreading views across half Somerset. The country beyond the lip of the hills is a high exposed plateau, with few woods apart from Rowberrow Warren, and was once the Royal Forest of Mendip where kings hunted stags from their Axbridge base.

If so sparsely populated an area can be said to have a capital, Priddy fills the part as well as anywhere, a small straggle of houses where many hilltop roads converge. Priddy, not surprisingly in view of its position high on the Mendip uplands, is noted for its clean fresh air. It is said that this was the origin of its famous August fairs, which began when the dreaded Black Death was ravaging the villages of the valleys among and beneath the hills; the breezy climate was believed to have a purifying property, making the gathering of crowds safer than in the milder vales. It is noted for prehistoric relics – though the whole area is riddled with tumuli and other evidence of ancient habitation – the chief being Priddy Nine Barrows showing on the skyline. Near Priddy is one of the most famous cave systems for properly-equipped explorers, Swildon's Hole, only safe for expeditions in dry weather. It was found as far back as 1901 but exploration is not complete owing to its difficult sumps and underground rock-climbs. Noted for its beautiful lime formations, Swildon's Hole is exclusively for the expert, and then only with a recognised group of speleologists. Many years ago a prominent Bristol caver threw a birthday party for fifty friends in Swildon's Hole, where the merrymakers enjoyed sherry and birthday cake, not in normal dress at a bar but in cavers' helmets 200 feet under the Mendips. It was not, for such a man, an odd choice; he had then descended the difficult Hole more than 250 times.

Lead mining was for about twenty centuries the Mendips' wealth, the industry being recorded from pre-Roman times and finally dying about a hundred years ago. The lead mines saw two heydays, in Roman days and again in the 18th century. The Romans worked a number of mines around Charterhouse and Priddy, and built the road across the hills to the coast for shipment of the lead. Large pigs of lead have been discovered hereabouts on which were engraved by Romans or their British workmen the names of Roman Emperors. Slaves, rounded up from nearby villages, were a profitable form of labour for building the roads, mining the lead, and dragging it to the sea and waiting trading vessels. From the Mendip mines came the lead that still lines the bottom of the Great Bath at Bath, and from the same hills came the lead piping carrying the water today. Puzzled as to why pipes laid nearly 2,000 years ago continued in use while those in a house 40 years old were in need of replacement, I questioned a plumber who chanced to make history his hobby. Plumbers believe, he said, that the 2,000-year-old pipes at Bath continue intact because the water flows eternally at the same temperature, instead of creating the strains of normal pipes subject to fluctuations of temperature outside and of the water inside them. Mendip lead was valuable enough to be shipped to many corners of the Roman Empire; before the war a drainpipe was discovered under an ancient road near Rome itself, and was sent for identification by experts. They decided that it came from the far-away Mendip hills.

Roman workers apparently enjoyed themselves after the long days at the mines, passing the time in gaming and gambling; dice of the period have been found all over the area. They also had the small amphitheatre still visible at Charterhouse where entertainments of some kind amused the soldiers of the Empire garrisoned far from sunny Italy.

Learning something of the story of Romanised Mendip helps us understand why many have no doubt that the Arimathea legends of Glastonbury have, like many other legends subsequently backed up by excavations and increased historical knowledge, some rock base of truth under the overlay of additional surmise gathered down the centuries. Joseph was himself a merchant and mine-owner; local lore actually identifies a Priddy mine as his. Where would such a man, a relative of Christ who was full of the wonders of the Crucifixion and Resurrection, most likely go if driven by the inner spirit to take the new Gospel to the world? Not to his own land, for the Christian church was already growing in an embryonic form there without his help. Most likely his second choice might be the land where his business interests had already lain, where he was known to influential men as well as the humbler populace as a man whose words were not idle dreaming. Surely the Mendip area must have sprung to mind, and on arriving back in Somerset with his eleven weary companions, what would strike them as a more natural place to land with the new religion than Avalon, from time immemorial a Celtic and Druidical place of worship? The landing at what we still call Weary-all Hill seems more likely when the historic context of Joseph's Mendip business connections is taken into account.

Priddy preserves one of the most thought-provoking of Somerset's legends: that when Joseph of Arimathea brought the youthful Christ to Britain he not only showed Him his local mine (natural enough in an owner escorting a visiting nephew), but that He possibly stayed on there for a while during those unrecorded adolescent years while Joseph returned to Palestine, picking Him up again on another voyage.

Hearsay alone? Many things even today are hearsay, told by mouth but not reported in print, especially localised incidents. Are they automatically foundationless for lack of documentary record? Mrs. Jones tells Mrs. Richards that her cousin has adopted a Welsh orphan; Mrs. Richards tells a third party who repeats that Mrs. Jones's cousin has adopted a Scottish orphan: the original fact has been varied, but the basic truth remains, that the lady did adopt an orphan. Thus word of mouth blends fact with variation; thus – if it be true that all stories have an origin somewhere – tales of long ago which sound unlikely may have that buried element of genuineness.

Much of our first five centuries of post-Christian history was indeed preserved in this way until in the 7th century Gildas wrote the first true English history. Most earlier written records were by Roman authors, foreign settlers judging through Roman eyes by Roman comparisons, needing to impress an Emperor with their cities and roads rather than the local people's lives and stories, much as in modern wartime reports each side claims to have won the same battle, or to have achieved something more impressive than the other.

Unsubstantiated this legend of Christ may be, then, but there is one specially significant factor about it: it is not localised like a figment of one man's imagination, but exists in several other places which, in those days, were very far apart. Also, two of the areas where it appears were given to Joseph of Arimathea's particular trades, tin and lead: Cornwall, long the centre of the tin trade, and Somerset, the Romans' great lead-mining district. They are separated by the whole of Devonshire, where the legend does not occur. This bears out the facts of the known trading route to western Britain; touching the tip of Cornwall, landing again in north Cornwall (where there is still a Jesus' Well), omitting Devon as it had no place in this particular commerce, and turning either towards the Brue for Avalon or, farther north, Uphill the Roman port for the Mendip lead shipments. So Joseph probably ordered his course, as today's businessman might stop at Rugby en route to Birmingham but omit Coventry as of no importance to his particular trade. A tall tale might be accepted in one area, but would it occur in two counties, completely separated by a third, and with reasonable consistency of outline?

Once arrived in Somerset's inland lagoon, a ship might follow a rectangular course: up the Brue towards Avalon, then across to the Mendips below Priddy, and along their feet back towards Uphill and the Channel; geographically the principal places involved tally. Whether pondered in a dispassionate historical/geographical light and regretfully rejected, or romantically and reverently with cautious acceptance, the thought of the adolescent Christ knowing Priddy, the Mendips and Avalon is a fascinating one.

The Middle Ages saw a revival of lead mining, reaching its ultimate peak in the 18th and 19th centuries. During Edward IV's reign a formal code of practice was drafted, laying down the boundaries of the mining area; requiring miners to be licensed; setting penalties for theft and other offences, including banishment "for ever"; and allowing for rescue in case of rock falls or other disasters. Victims were to be rescued and given Christian interment even though they might be "three score fathom under the earth". This code was superseded by an Enclosure Act of 1725, and since then the lead has been worked with more modern methods and equipment. A century ago a miner could earn over £1 for a day's work, when £2 was a week's pay for many wage earners. The ore, near the surface, was in earlier days extracted by digging, and the miners took plots by staking claims in a manner not unlike that seen in modern Western films. First the miner went to one of the Lords Royal for a licence before seeking out a piece of land as yet unworked. There he dug a pit about four feet deep and, standing therein, flung his tools with all his strength first to one side and then to the other; those points marked the boundaries of his plot, called a gruff. The resultant gruffy-ground (or, less familiarly, scruffy-ground) though abandoned is easily recognised by its uneven hummocks covered with rough grass. Victorian days saw a short burst of more mechanised activity that continued until just after the turn of the 20th century. Near Priddy and Charterhouse the abandoned buildings and flues stand forlorn and bleak. The many isolated inns on the plateau date from this time, being crowded then with gambling, cursing miners doing what their Roman predecessors did with their evenings – drinking and spinning dice. Will there be a third revival of the Mendip mines? They have died and come to life again more than once during the last two thousand years, so who knows?

Smitham Chimney is among the few major survivals of the 19th century's mechanised lead-mining days. It was repaired in 1919; funds were again badly needed in the 1970s, being sought among local residents, councils and commerce, with the object of strengthening and preserving this noted landmark and reminder of the past.

Shipham and Rowberrow, more to the north, again show evidence of gruffy-ground and closed lead mines. They also saw another mining industry rise, flourish and die, calamine being taken there for use in the zinc and brass trades. In the 18th century these villages were among the worst, socially, on Mendip, whose inhabitants had virtually abandoned all pretence at Christianity in their roughshod lives and manners. The squalor and lack of education for the children roused the wrath of the ubiquitous Hannah More to work for a revival of the half-dead faith, for better morals, and for the opening of Sunday Schools. The pioneer reformer's work was nowhere more sorely needed or more gladly given than at Rowberrow. Hannah More worked so tirelessly that nearly every Mendip village has some story to remember of her indomitable spirit; at least one has a road named after her, a Hannah's Lane.

This remarkable woman was born in 1745 near Bristol, her father being a village schoolmaster. After studying at a school run by her own sisters, she went to London and became involved in the theatrical world. Dr. Johnson and Garrick were among her friends, Garrick actually producing her play "Percy". Following Garrick's death she turned against the artificial theatrical and society world; religious writing became her new interest, together with a deep concern for the moral and educational conditions of her native West Country. Cheddar in particular shocked her with its ignorance, poverty and lack of guidance for the young, and there she started the chain of Sunday Schools through which invaluable work was done despite local opposition. Hannah More thenceforth became the great benefactress of Mendip, working tirelessly in life for local welfare and religious education, and in her will leaving no less than £30,000 to charities and religious bodies, a fortune then in 1833. Among her many tussles with local characters was the so-called Blagdon Controversy, born of the Blagdon curate's accusation that the head of a little school founded there in 1795 was holding suspect religious gatherings not in accordance with tradition. Such were Hannah More's obstacles, but posterity has recognised the worth of her work throughout the Mendip country.

Strawberry growing has for many years been the foremost calling on the south facing slopes, not only at Cheddar and Draycott but also round a number of other villages on the red-earthed central Mendips. In the picking season women work in the fields where the sun can be surprisingly hot and penetrating; in their protecting sunhats, crouching uncomfortably between the rows of strawberry plants doing back-breaking hand work, they are reminiscent of the women who labour in the swelteringly humid rice fields of northern Italy, except that the Somerset climate is infinitely kinder than the sticky unhealthy heat of the paddy fields.

The south slopes of the hills have many small but attractive villages worthy of a visit, Westbury-sub-Mendip, Rodney Stoke and Easton to name but three, not to mention Chewton Mendip on the plateau above Wells, for its notable 15th century church and its exceptionally fine tower. The plateau still mapped as Mendip Forest, albeit a forest with few trees and those lonely and windswept, is far from a minus mark after the hills' four tourist attractions between Wells and Axbridge have been eliminated. All that is needed to bring that strange open landscape to life is enough imagination to visualise our grandfathers' grandfathers swearing, digging, drinking and gambling their miners' lives away like the Romans before them, men whose children were guided into more gentle ways by the fearless Hannah More of the Sunday Schools, and to see even farther back in the mind's eye Somerset villagers dragging lead and building roads under the eyes of Roman masters.

How typical of Somerset of the paradoxes, that the hills that saw Britons become slaves should also, have been the birthplace of so moderating an influence in a hard-living mining world as the early Sunday Schools.

Burrington Combe

The Curate and the Cavemen

> Rock of ages, cleft for me,
> Let me hide myself in thee.

THESE lines are as familiar as the opening of "Jerusalem", the Glastonbury hymn of the mystic poet Blake. "Rock of Ages" also has a Somerset ancestry, the story of its creation appearing in every guide to the county but more rarely repeated elsewhere.

One day in 1762 a curate of Blagdon, Augustus Toplady, was rambling through Burrington Combe a few miles away, one of the smaller ravines that, like Ebbor Gorge, are less commercialised rivals of Cheddar. From a lowering sky the first spots of rain fell, spots that any local man would realise heralded more than a passing shower. A roll of thunder drummed across the darkening hollow as Toplady eyed the untamed scene for shelter. Luckily he was close to one of the larger rock masses, a solid rampart split at an angle almost from top to bottom by some spasm of nature many ages ago. Into the cleft the curate slipped, to shelter while the storm flashed, grumbled and showered its fury; he felt secure from the elements as the Christian is taught to feel safe in the Everlasting Arms. This nebulous idea began to take shape in his mind as the rain teemed down outside his shelter of age-old rock. Age old: a rock of great age: a rock of ages: so perhaps the wording took form and slipped into place: "Rock of ages, cleft for me, let me hide myself in thee".

To the accompanying splatter of rain and the rumbling of thunder, Toplady's words expanded into lines expressing a very opposite emotion: serenity. He had a pencil in his pocket, but not even a scrap of paper to jot down ideas he realised come but infrequently in such perfect form, words he must not forget on the long tramp home. All he could find was a playing card, and on its mundane surface he is said to have noted down the thoughts that were to be immortal in the English hymnody; the original card is reputed to be in existence somewhere on the other side of the Atlantic.

About forty years ago a tablet was let into the block of Mendip stone known as the Rock of Ages, marking the place where a country curate conceived one of our most enduring hymns: "This rock derives its name from the well-known hymn written about 1762, by the Rev. Augustus Montague Toplady, who was inspired whilst sheltering in this cleft during a storm". "Rock of Ages" has held its popularity through many generations and at all levels of religious belief from Non-conformist to High Church. It is understood to have been Gladstone's favourite hymn.

Once open-air services at the Rock of Ages were a regular feature of summer at Burrington Combe. Ironically, the first attempt at revival was abandoned on account of the very phenomenon to which the combe owes its fame: a heavy storm.

Burrington Combe is more than a human-interest association; in many eyes it has something the grander gorge of Cheddar partly lacks, at least during the height of the day in summer: wildness and peace. Tours to Cheddar often travel via Burrington, enabling passengers to glimpse the Rock of Ages, but few stop there. Those who do find the Combe are family motorists, people brought by country buses to the nearest roadside corner, or hikers about to prove their stamina by tramping from here over Mendip Top to Cheddar. Its beauty is smaller and softer than Cheddar's, the beauty of a graceful woman with a hidden tigress temperament. Concealed dangers lie all round Burrington, the district being notable for many caves and potholes ranging up to the maximum in difficulty and challenge, speleology being one of the leading adventure sports in northern Somerset.

Aveline's Hole holds one of the unsolved mysteries of Mendip, a mystery of fifty dead men. Their skeletons when found were so ancient that stalagmite had formed on their bones – and at Cheddar scientific measurement suggests that stalagmite growth is about 4,000 years to one inch. Who were they? Where did they come from, and why did they enter the cave, never to emerge alive? The macabre story is beloved of local tale-tellers, but neither they nor expert speleologists have so far found a really likely explanation of the fifty skeletons.

The largest cave, Goatchurch Cavern, has similar yarns woven about it, of men who became lost in its labyrinth of twisting passages and were trapped for ever under ground; one can only guess the horror of a lone man condemned to die of starvation in the web of intricate passages in the dark, damp bowels of Goatchurch Cavern.

Modern cavers use all the latest equipment; lights, ropes, diving gear, and protective helmets, descending in parties with the backing of effective cave-rescue organisations, and with proper training in caving techniques and stamina building. They have a wide choice of caves to explore, including some of lesser difficulty suitable for beginners near Burrington, though these do entail some climbing and crawling.

The cavers' map of Mendip shows some intriguing names, such as Rod's Pot and Drunkard's Hole. The more difficult caverns where explorers may meet with underground waterfalls, sudden floods, sheer chimney-like descents or uncertain footholds, take their toll occasionally, though there are few fatalities thanks to the combination of suitable equipment, adequate preliminary training, and the work of the cave-rescue groups. One of the few accidents to survive in local conversations with interested strangers happened in the famous Swildon's Hole, when an inexperienced explorer became too exhausted to negotiate a 35-foot-high underground waterfall on the way back to the surface. The waters were rising and the unfortunate caver was caught for some time amid the fall's full spate, dying of cold and exhaustion there. A lesser evil of Swildon's Hole is the Double Pots, where many an adventurer has taken an unwilling ducking, which is said to earn him the honourable title of a true son of Mendip.

Swallets abound around Burrington and on the hills above, including the St. Cuthbert's Swallet that has still not been fully investigated. Somerset men blessed with courage, good physique and an inquisitive mind are lucky to be able to indulge so widely in the challenging activity of speleology, both for the physical test it poses and for the hope that some unsuspected marvel may reward their explorations.

For ordinary mankind whose native habitat is above ground, Burrington Combe and the hills around it offer splendid walking country as well as picnic and recreation spots for the less active. The hillsides are a mixture of rock masses and rough grassy slopes and hollows, and the open ravine holds all the warmth of the summer sun.

An English hymn and a mystery of fifty dead men: Burrington Combe provides food for two very different trains of thought as well as scenery that has not entirely lost its rugged wildness in the motoring age.

The North Face of the Mendips
Fairy Toot and Fat Trout

FOR centuries in ancient times, much of central Somerset west of the Mendip Hills was occupied by a widespreading arm of the sea, whose exact nature we can now only deduce from topographical study, discoveries like the lake-villages, and a knowledge of similar enclosed lagoons and drowned estuaries elsewhere. The shallow water no doubt petered out into fens, marshes and tidal flats on its inner edges, being more open away from the hills and peninsulas. The last surviving stretch of the old watery Somerset disappeared only in the 18th century, when Meare Pool finally became pasture land along with the infinite miles of utterly level moorland we now see where the sea bed once lay. With the end of Meare Pool, Somerset ceased to be a lakeland county.

Only two centuries later, by one of those strange twists of destiny that are so noticeably a feature of the county, the waters returned, but under human control: indeed, at human instigation. During the twentieth century no less than three large sheets of water were created, one in the very area that once was largely submerged, the lakes of Blagdon, the Chew Valley, and Axbridge. The latter, as has already been mentioned, was created almost where the original lagoon met the central Mendips, on the edge of the present-day moors, enabling us to see the Isle of Wedmore once more rising above breeze-whipped wavelets, a more vivid demonstration of how the Somerset lakes looked than would be ours purely through description and imagination.

The other two human-made lakes are situated not where the ancient waters rippled, but on the other side of the hills amid gently rolling vales quite unlike any country we have so far visited.

Originally Blagdon was just another village, looking down on the valley of the little River Yeo, until the long and beautiful lake was made. The new Blagdon thereafter found itself achieving a modest fame and an influx of visitors, mainly those whose greatest delight is to sit motionless for hours on a lake bank watching for the telltale twitch of a rod and line. Since those early days, Blagdon Lake has become steadily better known, mainly for its large stocks of that desirable but elusive fish, the trout.

For non-anglers, too, Blagdon gained a new face with the coming of the lake, a face of increased natural beauty. The best views are from the surrounding hills, where the two-mile long lake snatches something of the blue above to vie with the green of valley meadows. A closer view may be had from the dam at the foot of the steep lane from Blagdon village; I well remember seeing it for the first time from that angle, in a misty morning haze that made the scene resemble the elusive shimmers of an Impressionist landscape, only the nearby reeds being in sharp focus against the indeterminate romantic mists hanging silently over the placid ripples.

The village, looking down on its picturesquely drowned valley, is dominated by the tall church tower; inside the church is a window in memory of the curate of Blagdon, Augustus Toplady, who joined the immortals with a single hymn written in nearby Burrington Combe, "Rock of Ages".

Only a couple of miles of country separate the Blagdon and Chew Valley lakes, making the district a veritable lakeland. The Chew Valley lake is about twice as big as its older neighbour, a huge sheet of shining waters. Like the Blagdon lake, it was constructed by flooding a large area of valley farmland, plus the site of a Roman villa and the course of a Roman road, though all but the most ardent historians agree that more was gained than lost. To look down from the gentle hills on this large and beautiful expanse of lake water in the heart of the green countryside is to see an already lovely area with a new focal point that shimmers and glitters from diamond-white to deep blue in a very English setting.

Fat trout are the most prized catch of the Chew Valley lake, as at Blagdon, attracting large numbers of hopeful anglers from a wide area, not least from Bristol whose urban sprawl, creeping ever nearer to Dundry Hill that stands like a protective bastion between the city and the meadows, now ends barely five miles away as the crow flies.

What kind of a land is this far side of the Mendips, the dip slope shelving towards Bristol away from the sheerness and bareness of the scarp slope that had all the tourist spots for itself until the advent of the two lakes? It is very different country, pastoral and rolling, undulating quietly for miles instead of falling to a clearly defined ending as at Cheddar and Axbridge.

It is old England, whose village names have the sound of Elizabethan verse about them: Nempnett Thrubwell; Hinton Blewett, Compton Martin; Chew Magna. Most of them have some point of interest, more likely to be discovered by pottering at random around the rural lanes than in a tourist guide, but a few may be mentioned for their special associations.

Wrington is most interesting from the human viewpoint, one of the most interesting places, having associations with not one but several outstanding people. John Locke, the philosopher, was born at Wrington, and Somerset's most famous social reformer, Hannah More, lived there. At Wrington she entertained such figures as Dr. Johnson and the man who brought the freedom of slaves to reality, Wilberforce. With her sisters, she is buried in Wrington churchyard. Richard Whiting, the man who was to become Glastonbury's last Abbot and one of the sacrifices of humanity on the gallows of the Reformation, was also born there. Beatified centuries later for his martyrdom, he is thus on the road to possible canonisation; should that day ever come, Whiting would be a saint of Wrington as well as Glastonbury.

Music owes something to a rector of Wrington, and the village was also the last resting place of the man whose stature was sufficient to take him to the post of Master of the King's Musick, following no less a man than Elgar.

The first of Wrington's two musicians was the Rev. William Leeves, composer of the music of the popular ballad "Auld Robin Gray", but his light is rather overshone by that of Sir Walford Davies who died at Wrington in 1941. Davies was a distinguished teacher and organist as well as a composer, who had held two of the most exalted posts in the British organ world, the Temple Church in London and St. George's Chapel, Windsor. His compositions included a symphony, a number of large-scale chord and orchestral works, overtures, suites, anthems and chamber music, but he is remembered now chiefly for two works, both short but in their own forms close to perfection; he is at least spared the indignity of becoming after his death what musicians scathingly call a one-work-composer, the short but exquisite anthem "God be in my Head" being almost as well known as his only other regularly performed composition, the "Solemn Melody" that is an undying part of Britain's musical heritage.

In his lifetime Sir Walford Davies was occupied as much by teaching as by composition. As professor of music in the University of Wales he came into specially close contact with students' uninhibited hymn singing, and was already pondering a request that he should produce a hymnal for their use when a similar suggestion came from the Student Christian Movement. "Hymns of the Kingdom" was the outcome, a collection of brisk and lively tunes old and new. Davies' preface reveals the writer of "Solemn Melody" as in general opposed to solemnity in worship: "Music is a stream of living history" he wrote, the vital word being "living", not rooted in a stolidly pious past without concessions to the present. Something of the Salvationists' cheerful religion comes over in his comments: "Even hearty laughter and heavenly pursuits are quite compatible", and – of Amens – "Pretend you may never sing another, and put everything into it".

Hymn tunes, incidentally, are traditionally identified by very brief titles, often of only one word, placenames being specially popular. Thus nearly every English county is represented in our many hymnals, and Somerset is no exception; organists from Cumberland to Cornwall are familiar with such tunes as "Blagdon", "Mendip", "Midsomer Norton", "Avalon", "Wells" and "Glastonbury".

Continuing on music and musicians, that great favourite of drawing-room ballad days, "Green Hills of Somerset" comes readily to mind; a famous soprano recording made back in the "78" days can still bring a Somerset exile near to tears.

With the revived interest in the Victorian and Edwardian periods today, the serious compositions of such men as Parry are being rediscovered, on disc if not yet in the concert hall. Two of his works, however, have never lost their place, even through the anti-Victorian period that has now passed: "Blest Pair of Sirens", and his immortal setting of Blake's Glastonbury Hymn or "Jerusalem", which has been well used from the church to the Proms, though not all who sing it are aware that it refers to a particular story of "England's green and pleasant land". The Avalon legends would appear ideal operatic material in the "Lohengrin" vein; Martin Shaw, chiefly known for his rousing hymn tunes and as a co-editor of "Songs of Praise", did in fact produce one, "The Thorn of Avalon", bringing together such diverse characters as Arthur, the Archangel Gabriel, Sir Bedivere, Sir Lancelot, and of course Joseph of Arimathea. It was first performed in 1931, a long way from Avalon – at a Toc H Festival at the Crystal Palace.

Holst, of Swedish ancestry but born at Cheltenham, showed a West Country influence in "Egdon Heath", powerfully translating into music the feeling of Hardy's poetry. He had a special interest in English folk-song, harmonising and arranging many regional tunes. Some of these he incorporated into his best known work based on folk-song, the "Somerset Rhapsody".

Perhaps the most extraordinary musical project in Somerset was the attempt by the composer Rutland Boughton to make of Glastonbury an "English Beyreuth" with regular cycles of grandiose operas on native themes presented in the spirit of the great Wagner "Ring" cycle. Somerset undoubtedly had the basic material for such a venture in the Arthurian legends (Wagner, indeed, had turned to the English West Country himself for the story of "Tristan and Isolde", based on Cornish history) and Boughton certainly had the requisite enthusiasm.

A series of festivals were mounted, beginning in 1914 with a Glastonbury Festival with the modest Town Hall serving as opera house and a single piano deputising for an orchestra. Sadly, for various reasons, Glastonbury never became a rival to Beyreuth, nor was the grandiose projected opera house ever built. Rutland Boughton is now remembered only for his exquisite "Immortal Hour"; the West Country operas are known only to musicologists, and that chiefly by name alone: "The Queen of Cornwall"; "The Birth of Arthur"; "The Round Table".

Churchill, not far from Wrington, has relics of a far distant age to show, the large hill fort on Dolebury Hill. It dates back to the Iron Age, and is of outstanding size and interest, as well as a magnificent viewpoint commanding much of the seaward Mendip country.

Congresbury is not strictly a Mendip place, belonging more properly to the countryside inland from Weston and Clevedon, but as it falls within Axbridge's vast administrative area mention may be justified on two counts. Firstly, the church has a very unusual dedication (to St. Congar, the son of an Emperor of Constantinople, who, like Joseph at Avalon, planted his staff in the earth, creating not a Holy Thorn but a huge old yew) and a curious landmark tower crowned by a shorn-off truncated spire. Secondly, pottery found during digs at a 5th or 6th century earthwork which may overlay earlier work is believed to be of Mediterranean origin – and from the Mediterranean came Joseph of Arimathea among other lead merchants. So another little fragment of the combined jigsaw of history and legend is added.

From around Congresbury and Yatton the northern Mendip bulwark shows above the foothills, with Crook's Peak as a focal point. A sharp tooth-shaped nick shows on the high tableland as if some peckish giant had taken a passing bite, marking the topmost cliffs of Cheddar, partly obscured by intervening heights. Old cottages and outbuildings constructed sideways-on to the road, and the first stone walls hung with tiny ferns, tell those who love Somerset: "You're nearly there". "You are home!" sings Congresbury's strangely shaped tower, marking the entrance to the lost Cheddar Valley Railway of the happy memories.

Butcombe, near Blagdon Lake, is a very ancient village whose history stretches back to before Domesday; its setting in a narrow vale north of the lake is exceptionally pretty. Like all the Mendip country, its surroundings are rich in tumuli, barrows, and other remains of long-dead peoples of pre-history. Two large barrows of the Bronze Age stand close to the village, the larger of them having the delightful name of Fairy Toot. How a grave came to have so poetic a title I have not so far discovered, but it is worth recording for its sound alone. Fairy Toot – there is a world of imagination and delight in just repeating the name. A fairy with a hangover? A mystic aerial trumpeter summoning the buried to fairyland for ever? Probably something much less romantic, but it is a name not easily forgotten. Some, on the other hand, may find the intriguing placenames on the north Mendip map amusing; and why should one not be amused in so rural and Old English a countryside? The air of peace about the gentle hills, so unlike the rather severe south face of the range, is capable of relaxing the most tense townsperson in a few easy-going days. Even the chickens at the farm gates seem to cackle in hennish delight and the joy of living to lay egg after egg; even the cows have an extra placidness as they unhurriedly plod from tuft to tuft of grass; even a horse poking his face over a fence to neigh a greeting appears rather to be laughing because life on the quiet back-slopes of the Mendips is good.

Driving out from Bristol or Bath, this undulating agricultural countryside strikes the newcomer in a deceptive way. Milk churns stand by field gates, cows solemnly chew life away, and the road plunges into deep leaf-shaded lanes towards Chewton Mendip whose ornate church tower stands boldly silhouetted against the afternoon sun. Interesting but unfamiliar names appear on the signposts, such as

Hollow Marsh or Temple Cloud. Temple Cloud: the name is a two-word poem though the place itself is long, stone built, and solid. Can this be the Somerset of Arthur, Alfred, the Witch of Wookey, the saints of Avalon and the bloodstained field of Sedgemoor? Where are the dramatic ravines hewn from the hills, the caverns, the tourist spots, the wide views across an infinite flatness to the horizon, the medieval towns, and legendary Glastonbury?

The north-Mendip world is none of these, but another facet of a many-sided county, as if the countryside deliberately played itself down to heighten the impact of breasting the hills and seeing the heart of Somerset below. At the same time, the district springs one of the surprises that are part of Somerset's character, a colliery in a pastoral country, where cows graze near disused tips that nature has clothed with greenery as though to hide scars inflicted on her by mankind.

Like the East Kent and Forest of Dean coalfields, the Radstock colliery is one of the handful of small coalfields in southern England. Only discovered in the 18th century, it was supplying coal in bulk and employing more than 6,000 early in the 20th century. Gradually, with the advent of other means of power, the pits closed.

And so the road goes on southwards towards Wells, reaching the lip of the Mendips at last – and still there is no sight of Wells, the city that is the base for so many people's first exploration of central and northern Somerset. The sign "City of Wells" appears, but the road is completely rural; nothing could be less like a city approach. Suddenly, with a theatrical flourish, the curtain of green trees parts to reveal a scene almost too perfect to be real: the towers, battlements, ancient walls and mellow colours of the West Country's loveliest cathedral and city, shining calmly in the westering sun, as though it had all appeared from nowhere at the wave of a magician's wand. The long drive from the cities has ended at the threshold of medieval Wells, from which all the highlights and byways described in the last fifteen chapters are easily explored.

So ends a journey through smiling Somerset, a journey that started with Glastonbury of the saints, travelling across the silent moors to the coast, from the coast to the Mendip uplands and the places where Romanised slaves mined lead for the mighty Empire that once held sway over Britain. If but one reader has discovered something more in Wells than its central cathedral, accepted something of the spirit that Glastonbury and its Holy Thorn have been weaving into the hearts of men for centuries, or has been persuaded to wander off the tourist track in search of the lonely beauty of the moors, then putting such a journey into words and thence into printer's ink will have been a rewarding as well as pleasurable venture.

Conclusion

CONTRAST is Somerset's keynote, the introduction to this volume suggested, before going on to discuss as many aspects as possible of an exceptionally varied county: Glastonbury where Christianity's first light was lit; the moors that are scarcely noticed by passing travellers yet hold secrets of man's earliest existence among the ancient mires; the popular tourist places and some of their sidelights; three major industries developing alongside age-old farming activities; and the soul-tranquilising scenes that once witnessed the carnage of Sedgemoor, the Civil War and the Bloody Assize.

If the county is diverse, so are the people woven into its story. There are the saints, and the ruthless men who put Glastonbury's last Abbot to humiliating death; Roman slave-drivers, farmers, seaside donkey-men, builders of industrial empires, good King Alfred and Monmouth the pretender; rebels and martyrs, good men and bad.

Human activity, too, shows unexpected twists and turns. And how many counties see more tourists than does Somerset in Cheddar, Wookey Hole and Wells, and yet preserve such stretches as the turbaries or the Isle of Wedmore virtually untouched by the sightseeing herd?

Beliefs range widely, from Quakerism to the Benedictine Rule resurrected at Downside, from Celtic rites on Glastonbury Tor to the legends of Joseph of Arimathea. Some believe that One greater than Joseph may have trod Somerset earth in youth, a belief held by humble folk down the centuries until Blake summed it up for a wider world in one of the immortal works of English verse, familiar to a still larger number of people in Parry's equally undying musical setting:

> And did those feet in ancient time
> Walk upon England's mountains green?

Archaeology has backed up rather than destroyed several legends and theories of the past. Maybe some day this one, too, will be given a more concrete substance than words. Meanwhile we can reverently assimilate the possibility when walking the hallowed ground of the Avalon that is now called Glastonbury. The clinging intangible atmosphere about the Abbey's roofless nave, once it enters the receptive mind, is reason enough to call the place that is the heart of central Somerset a Jerusalem in "England's green and pleasant land".

Acknowledgements

NOBODY learns more from a book than the author in writing it; for every fact followed up or cross-checked another byway of history is opened, or another hitherto forgotten incident recalled.

Memory is not enough when dealing with facts. Inevitably the writer must turn to further sources for confirmation of impressions or for up-dating of information. Invariably he or she meets with painstaking help from numerous individuals, as I have discovered in the present project.

In particular I sincerely thank The Abbot of Downside; Mr. H. W. King, Director of Publicity, Weston-super-Mare; Mr. G. Robertson, Manager of Cheddar Caves; Mrs. O. Hodgkinson, Wookey Hole; Mr. H. F. Scott Stokes, F.S.A.; Mr. D. M. Cursley, Town Clerk of Wells; Dr. R. D. Reid; Mr. H. Tavener of Showering's and Mr. H. R. Burnard of Eric Buston & Associates Ltd. for help in the section on Babycham; Mr. Vernon C. Smart of Clark's for his advice, information, and setting in motion of further trains of thought; Morland's of Glastonbury for adding to my interest in sheep and sheepskins; Mr. W. J. Harvey, Entertainments and Publicity Manager of Burnham-on-Sea, for confirming and expanding my knowledge of the Parrett Estuary; Mr. B. D. C. Totterdell, Street Librarian, for confirming certain elusive points; Mr. F. K. C. Adams of Axbridge Rural District Council for his helpfulness on archaeological matters; the National Maritime Museum library for courteous research on the Parrett flatner; Mr. M. Butlin, Keeper of the British Collection at the Tate Gallery, for equally minute research; the libraries of the Victoria and Albert Museum and National Gallery; the very painstaking public libraries of Bridgwater and Wells; Stuart Mitchell for helpful suggestions and, by publishing much of my earlier writing, enabling me to spot its weak points in print; Mrs. J. Clayton for additional anecdotes; Sir Arthur Elton of Clevedon Court; the Headmaster of the Kings of Wessex School; my Mother for reviving certain schoolday memories, and my Father for giving us six years of country life. Last, but certainly not least, my thanks to Somerset for being Somerset, a county of such individuality that only several volumes could do true justice to its variety of scene and unmistakable personality.

MURIEL V. SEARLE.